UNDERCOVER

ONE OF THESE THINGS IS ALMOST LIKE THE OTHERS

BASTiEN CONTRAiRE

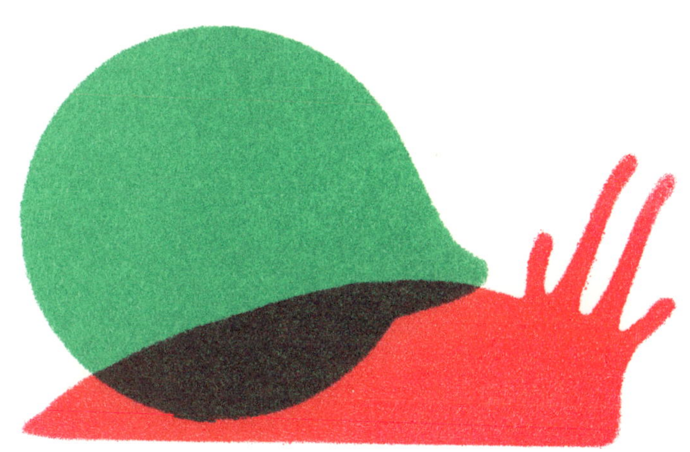

Φ

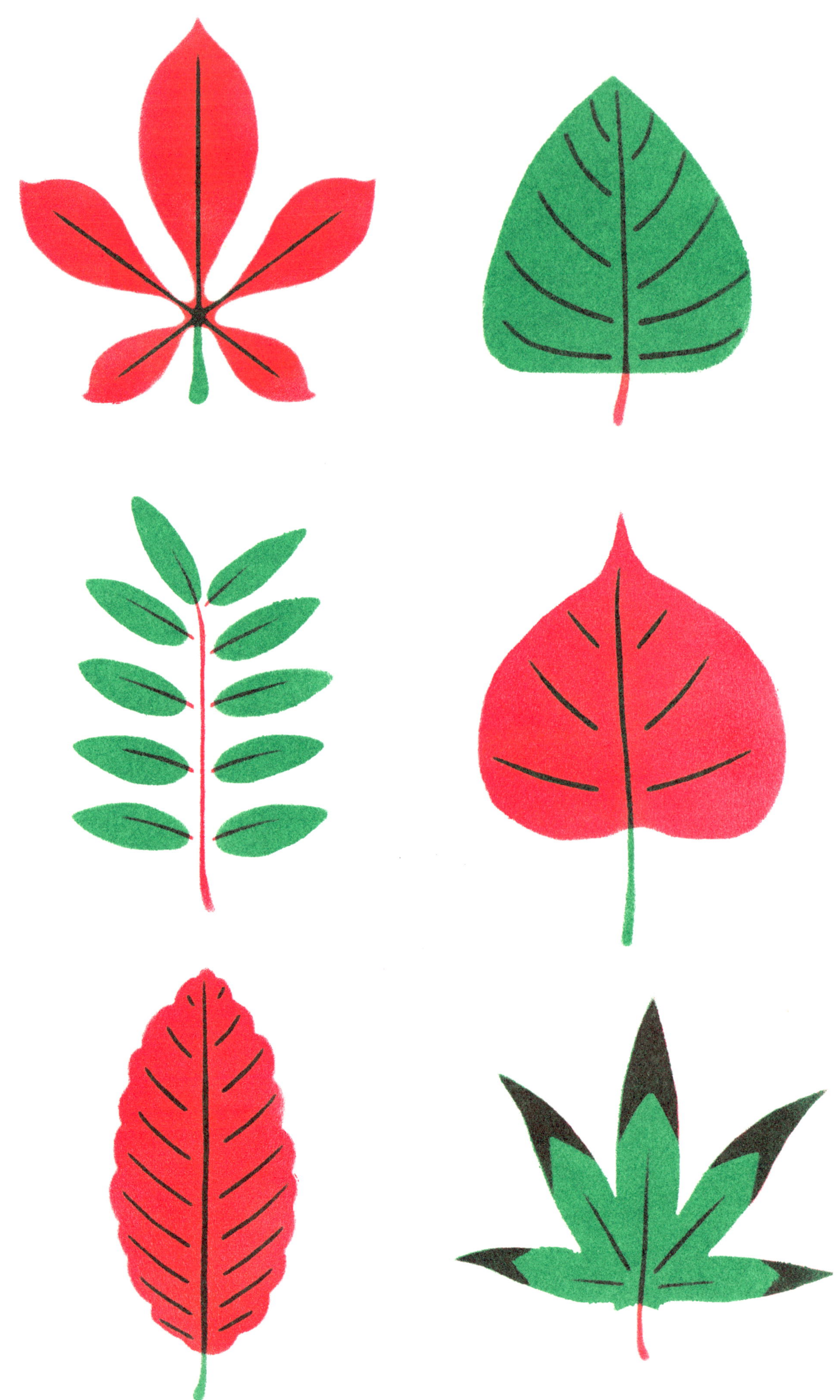

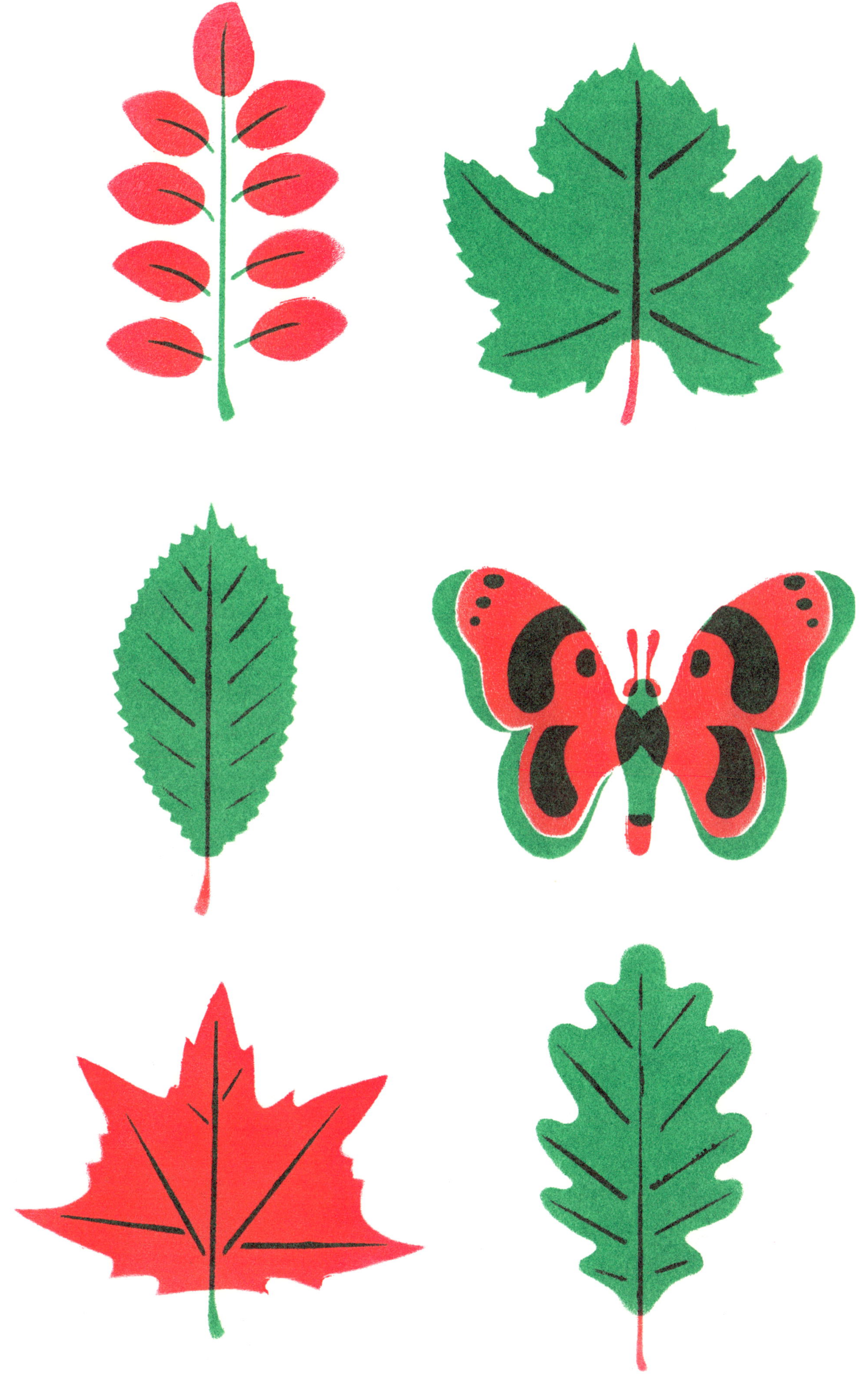

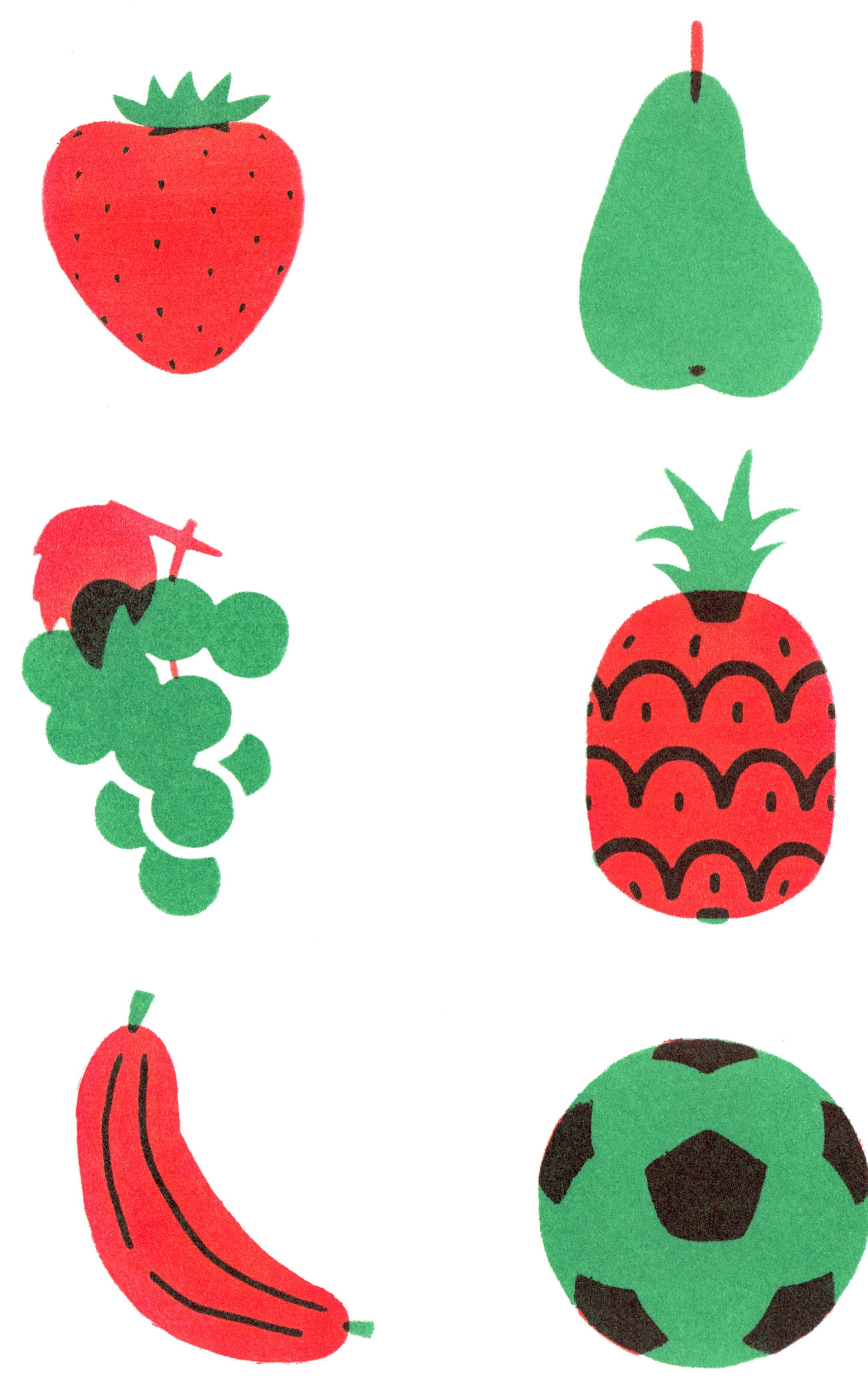

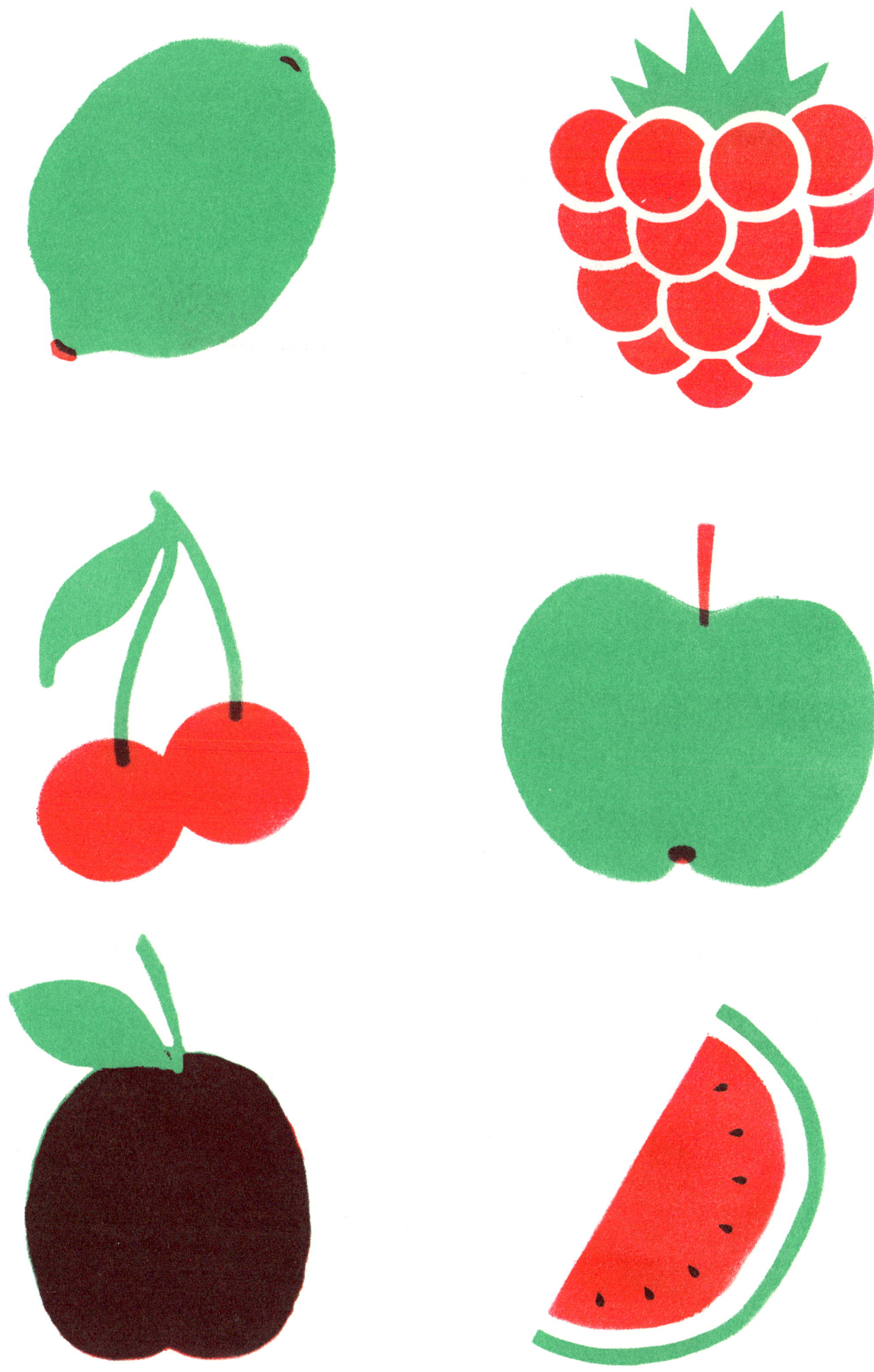

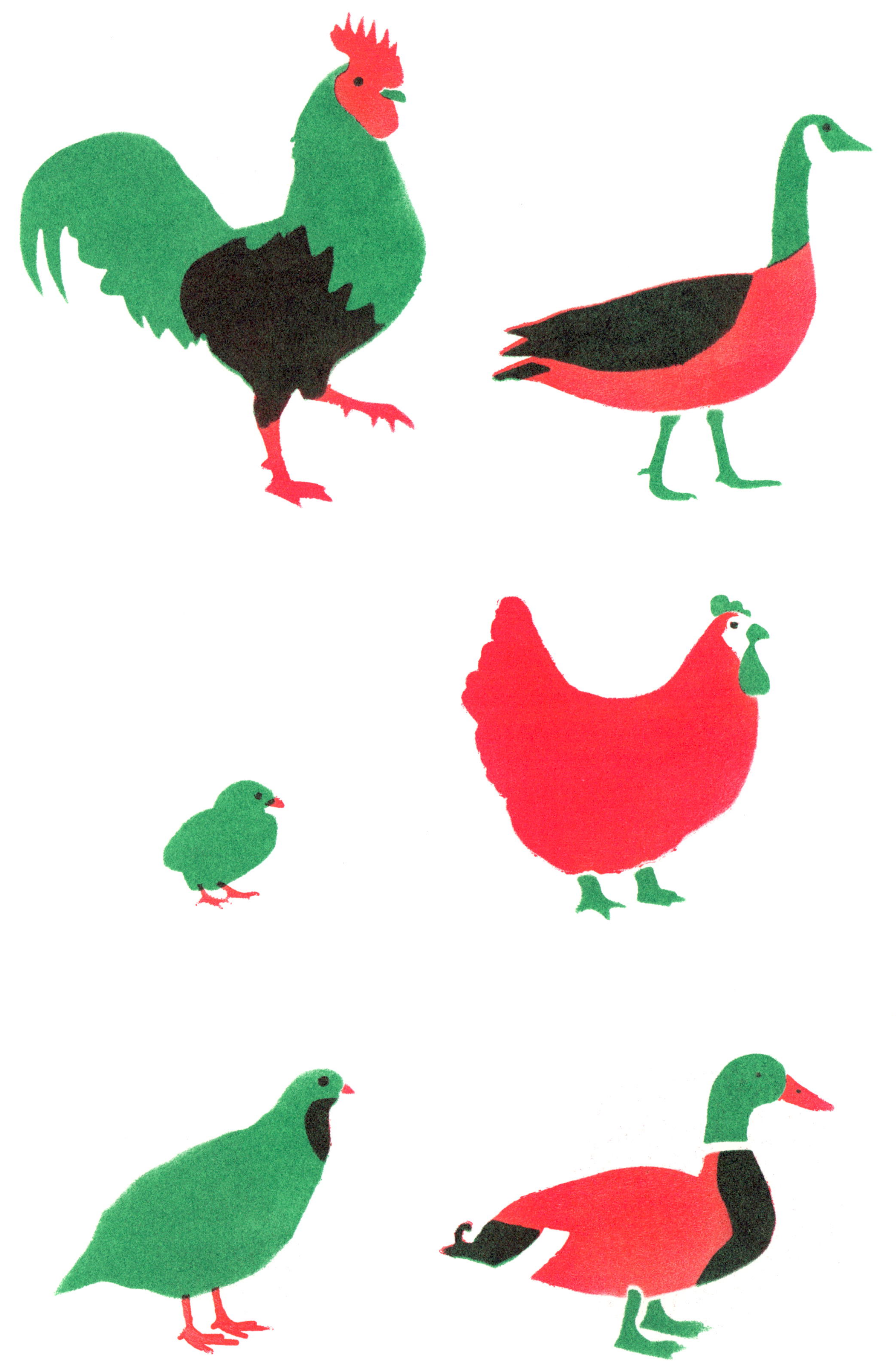

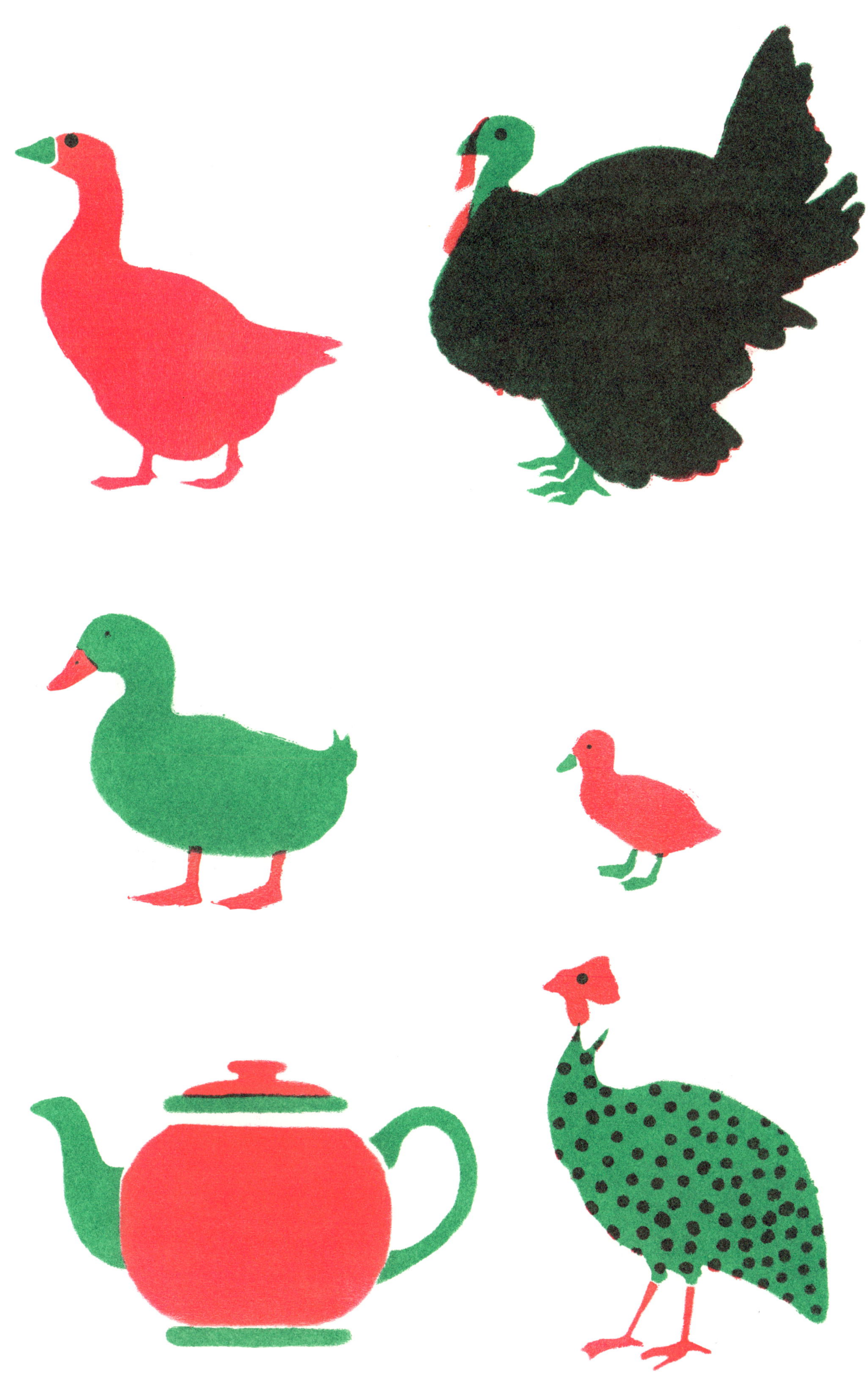

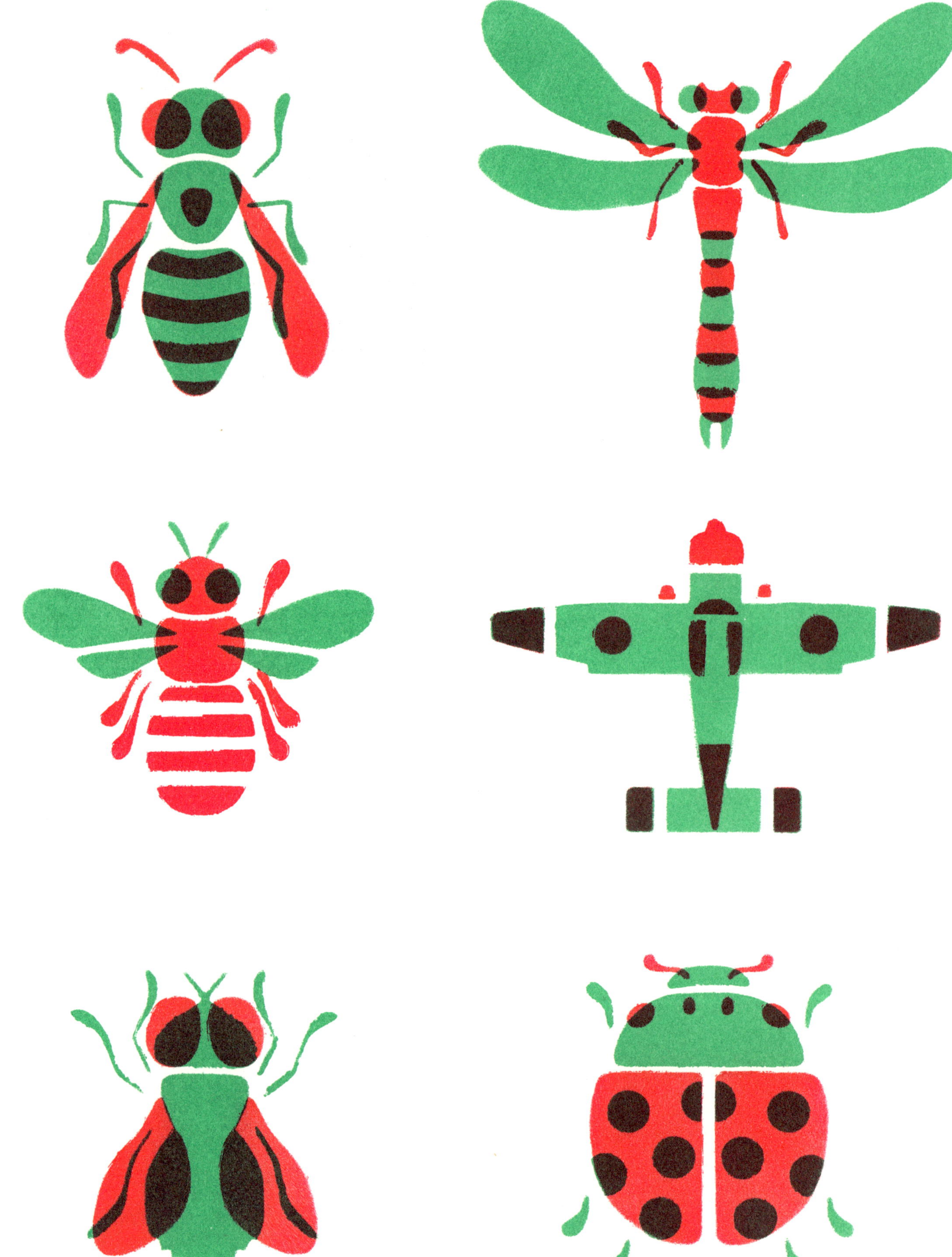

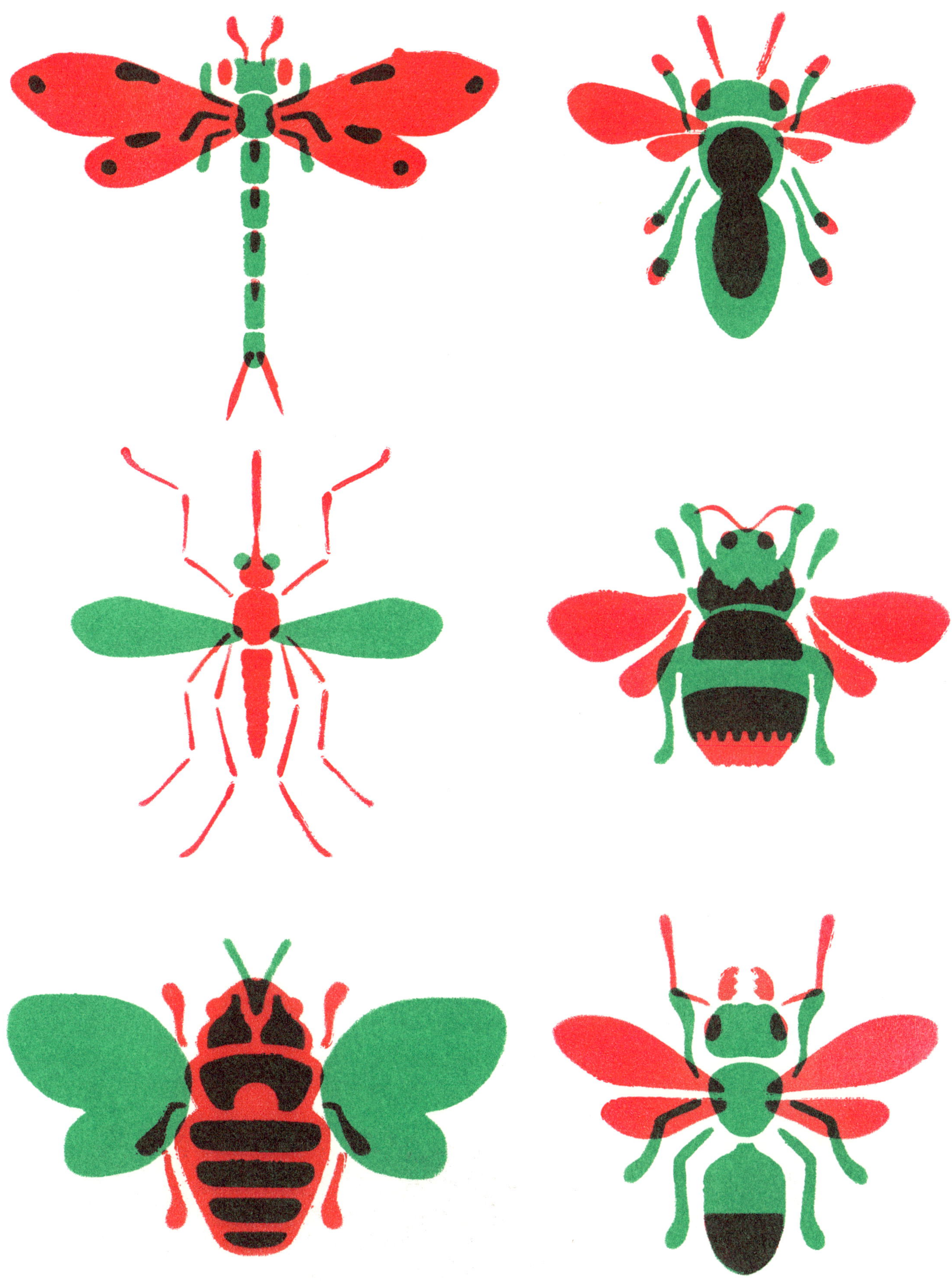

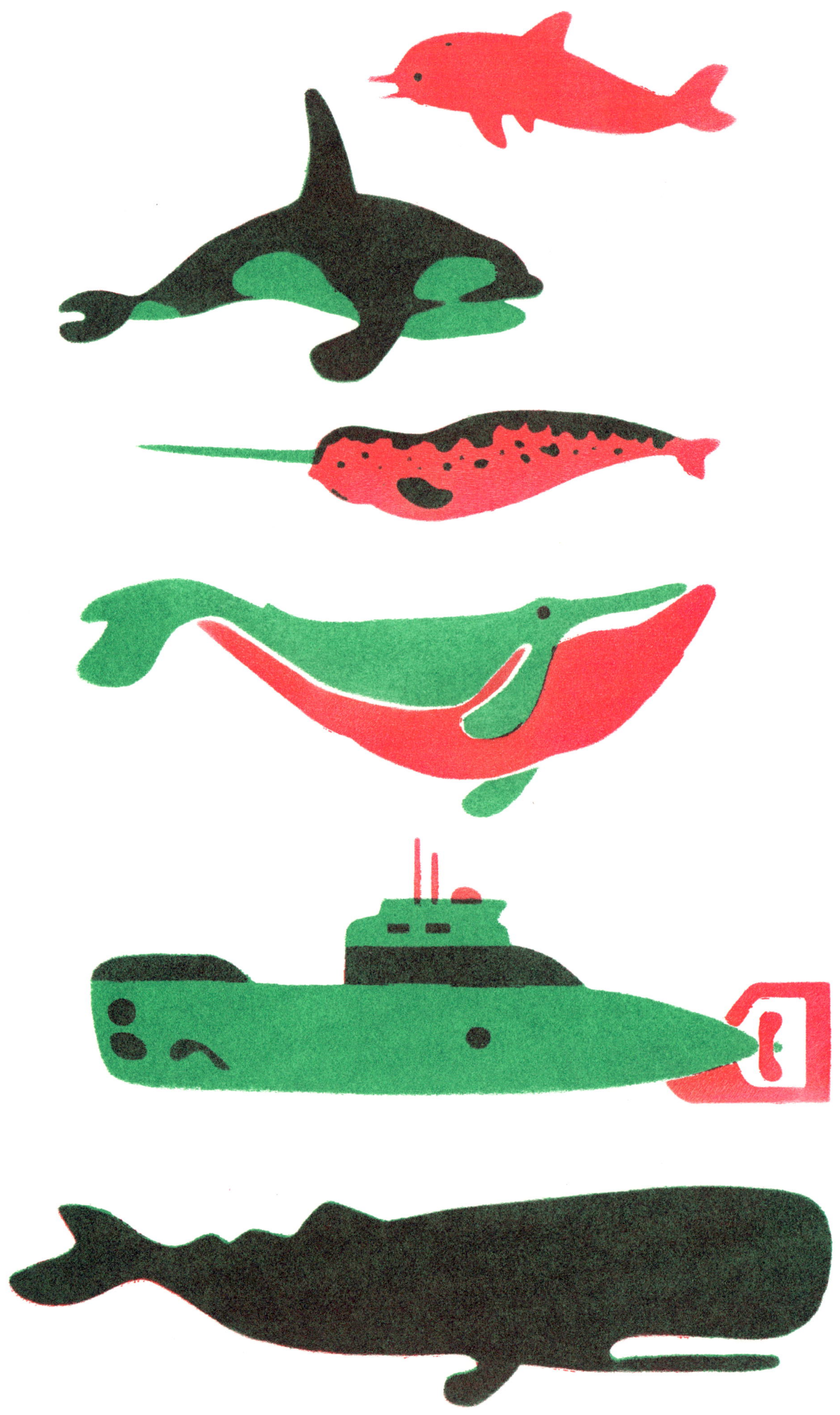

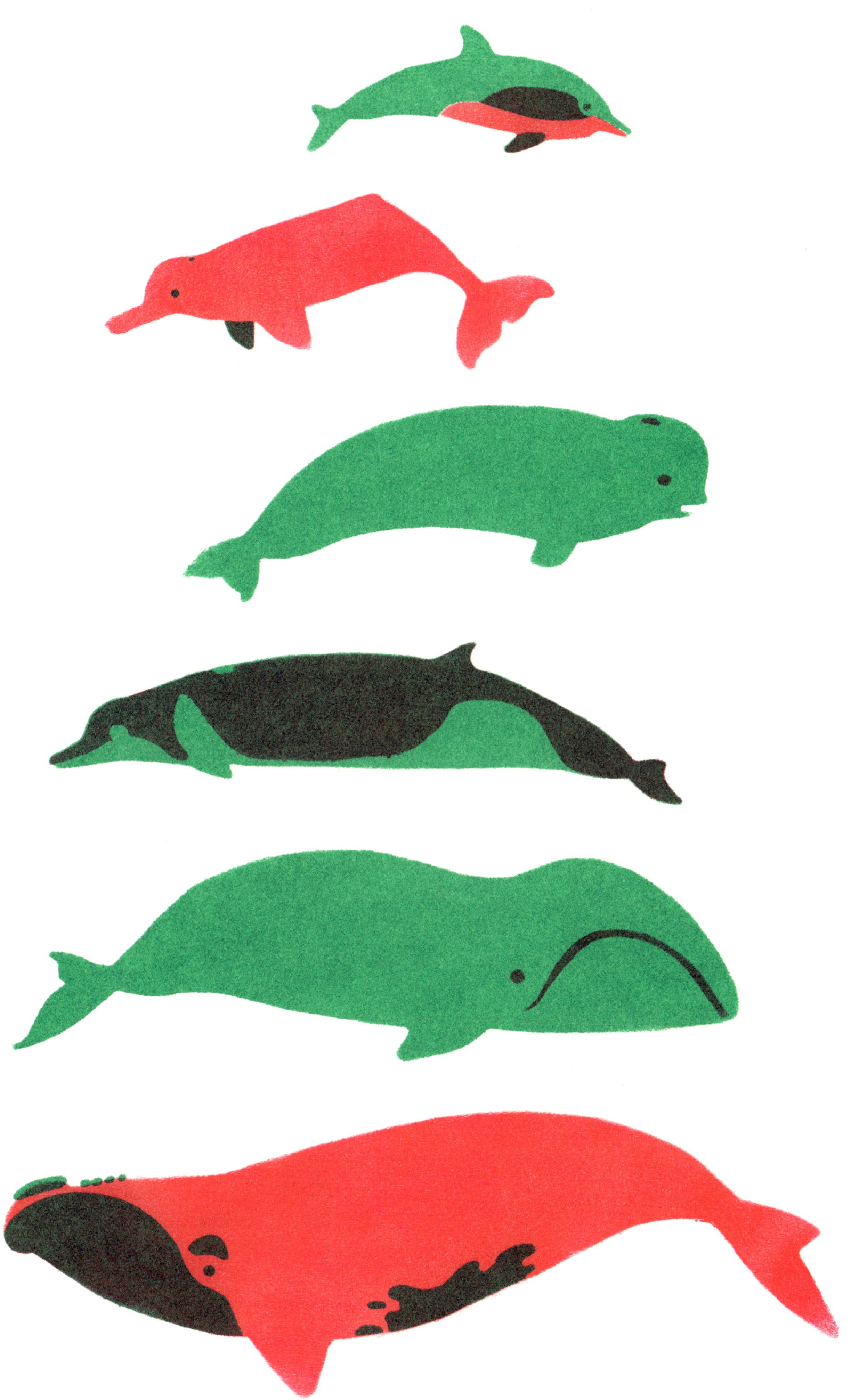

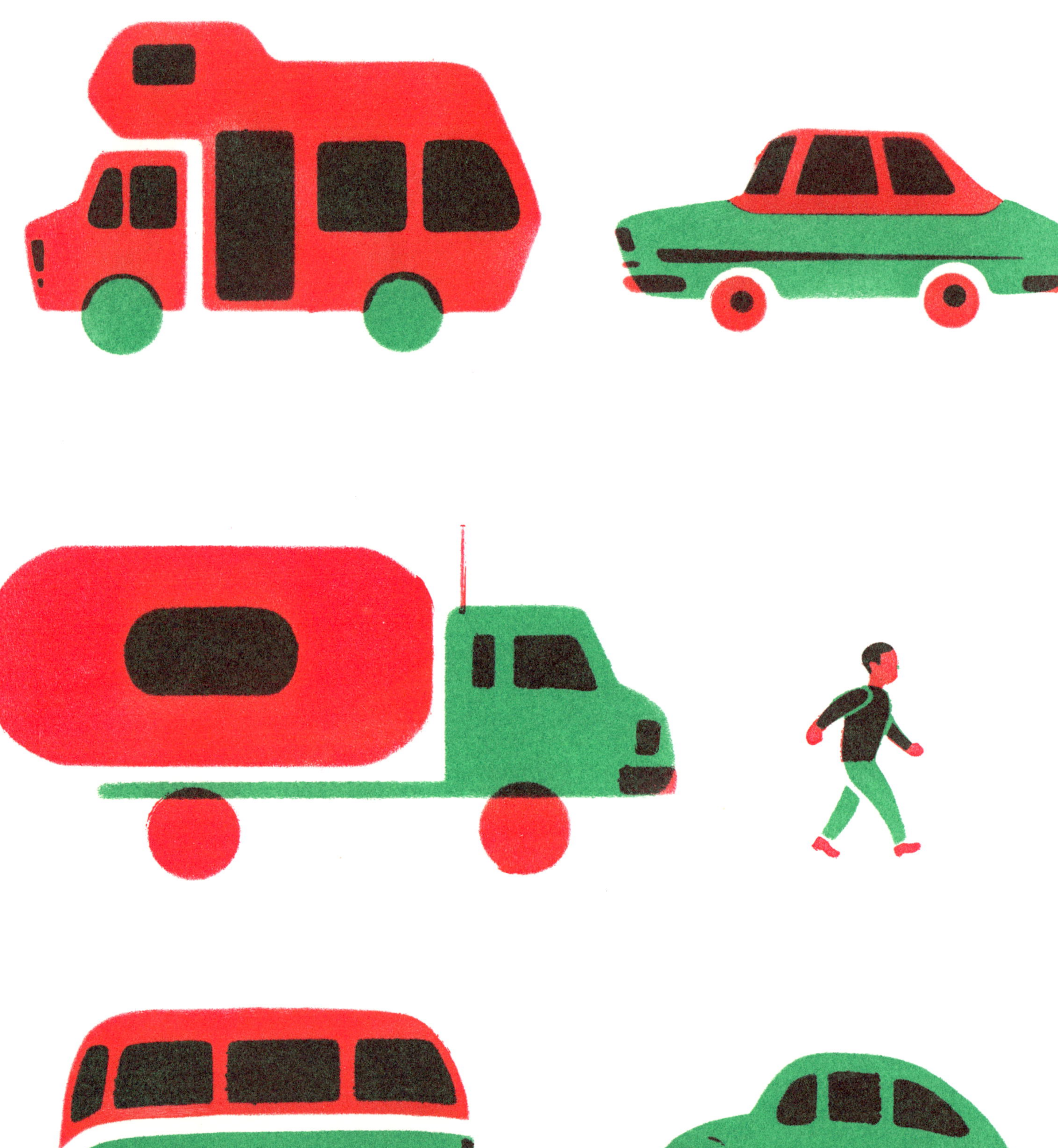

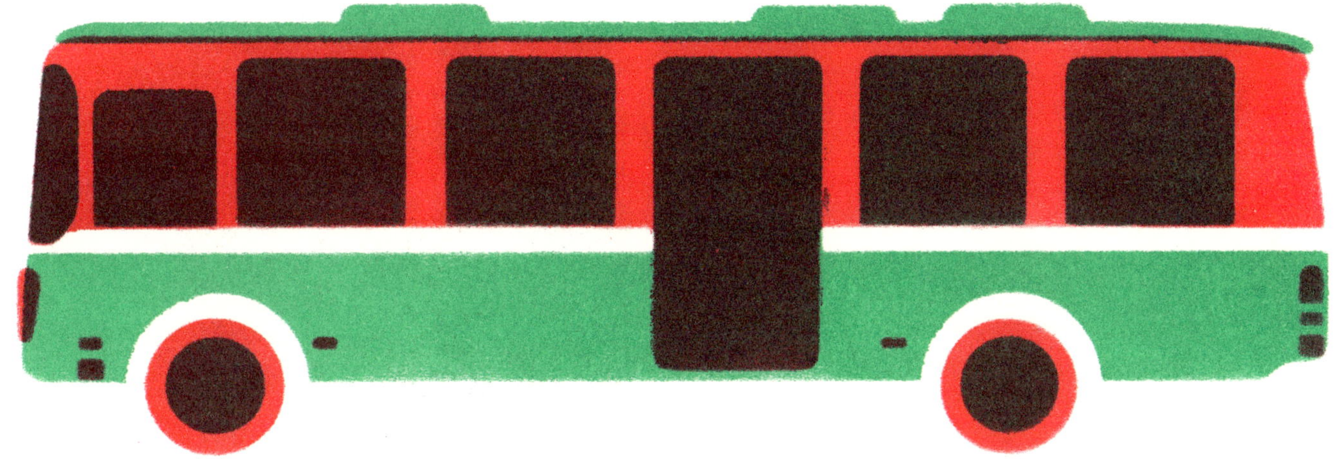

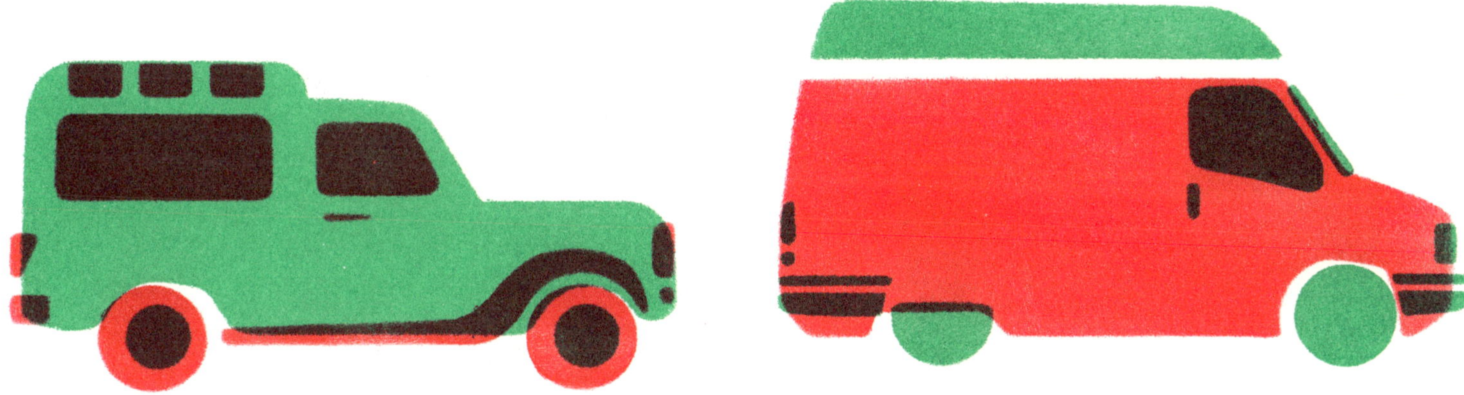

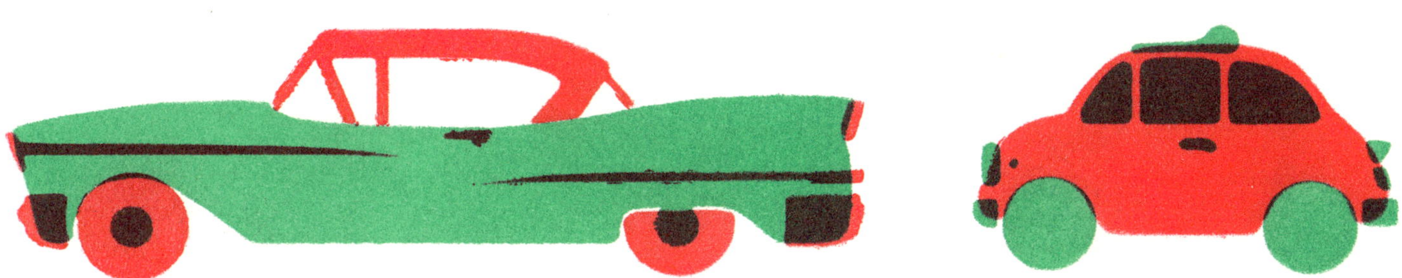

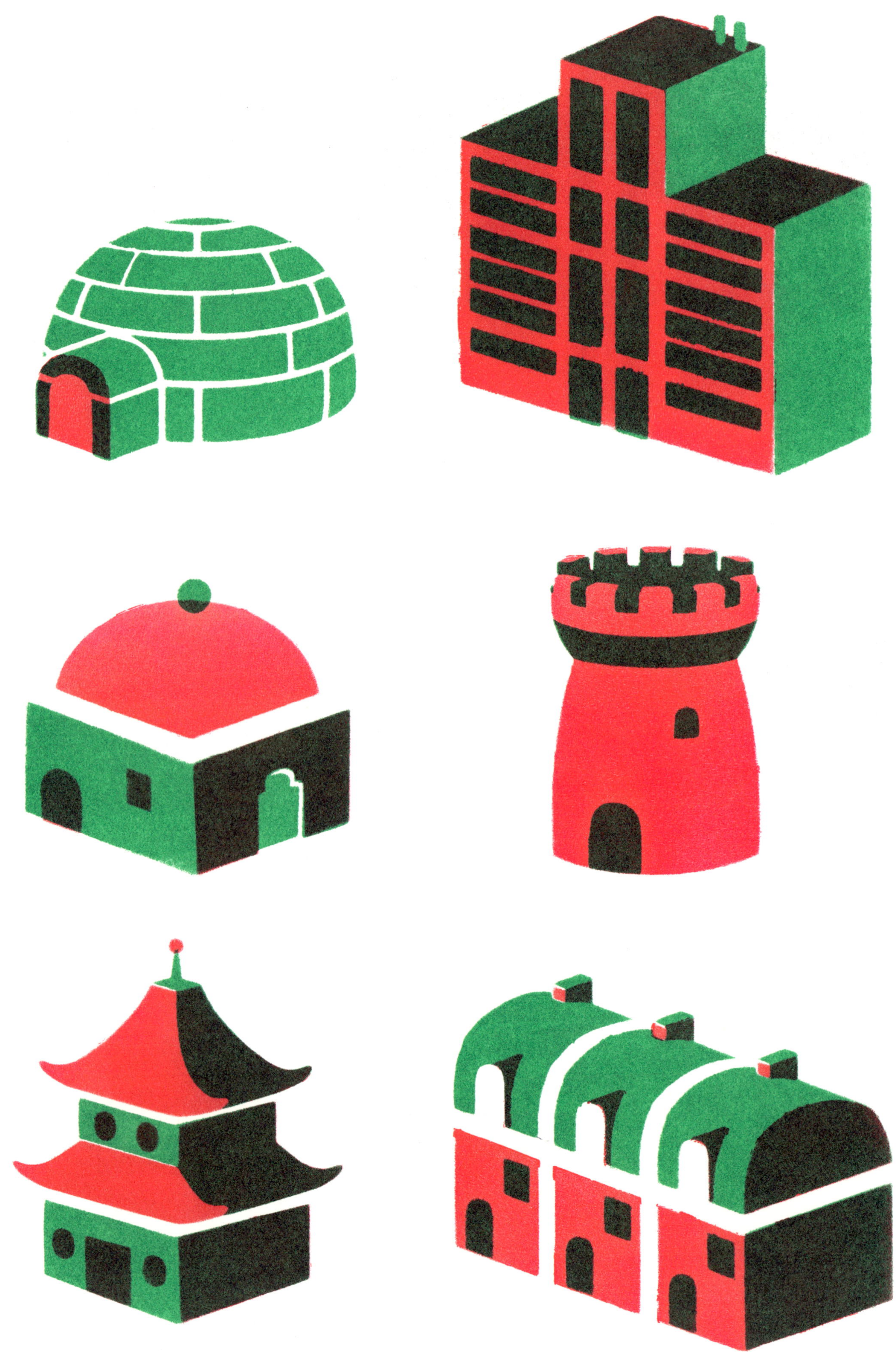

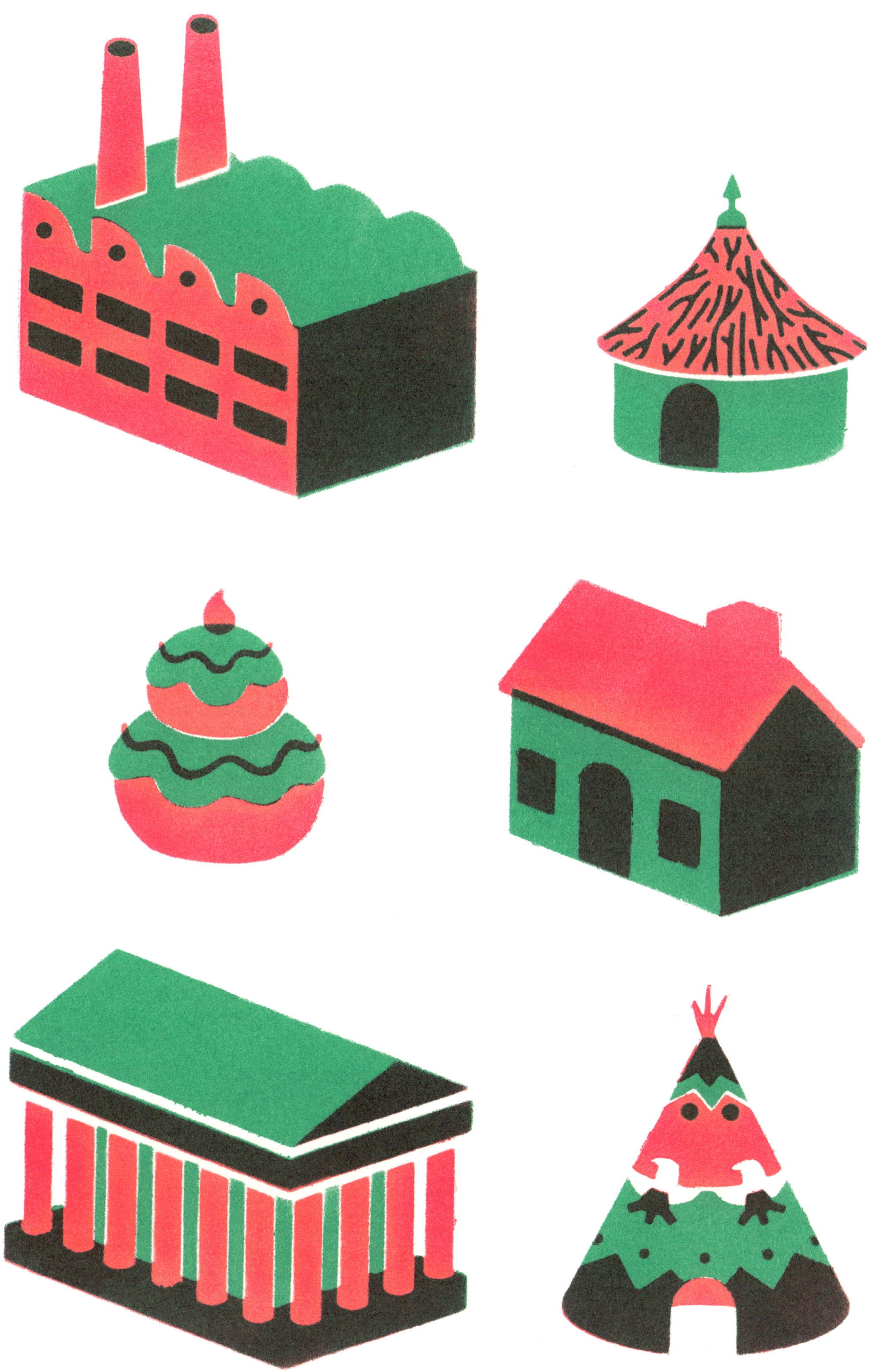

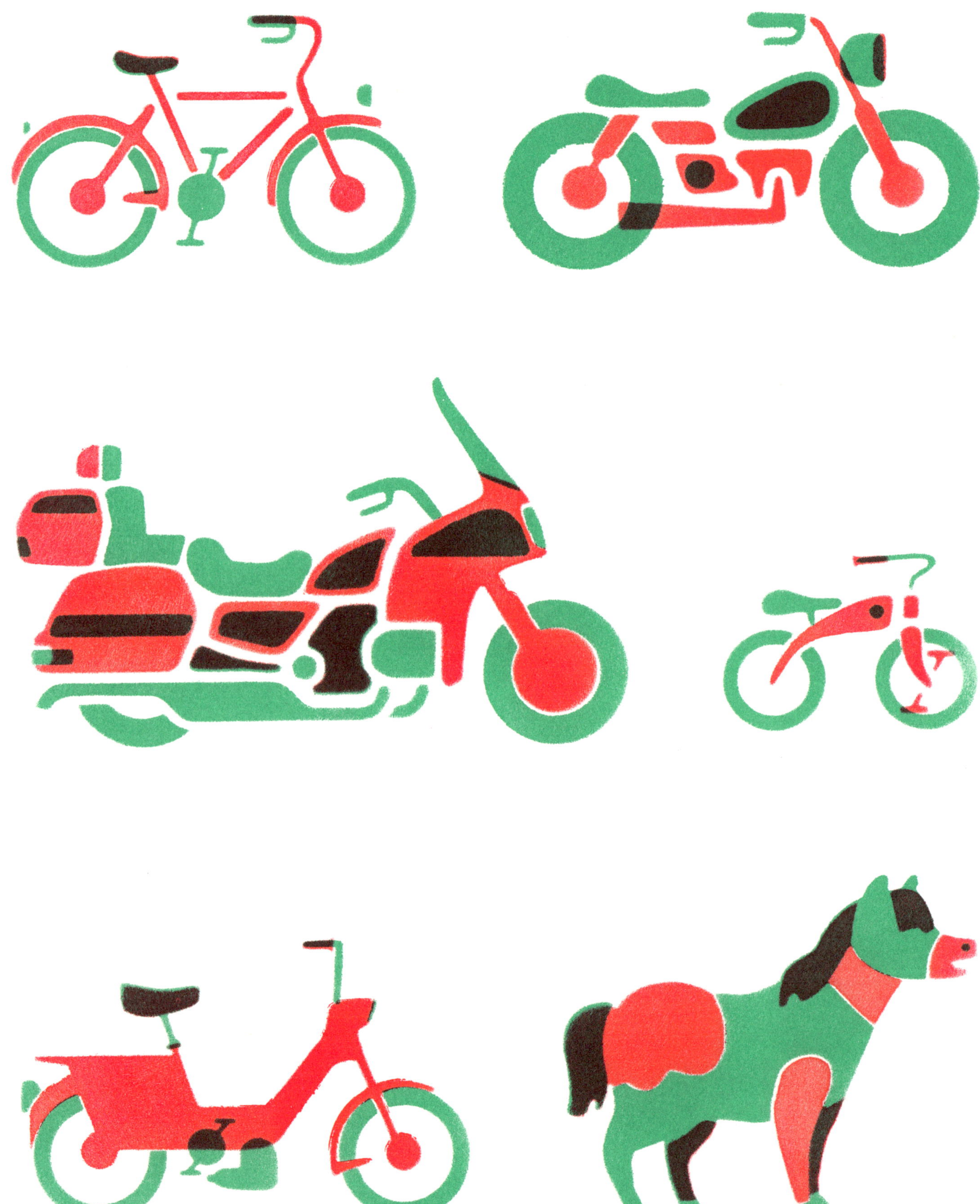

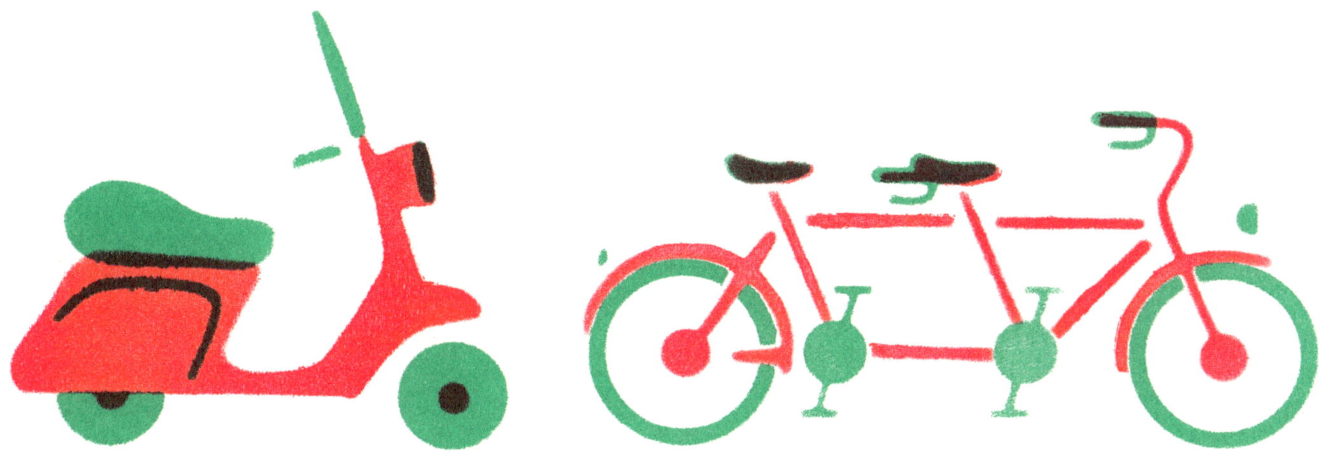
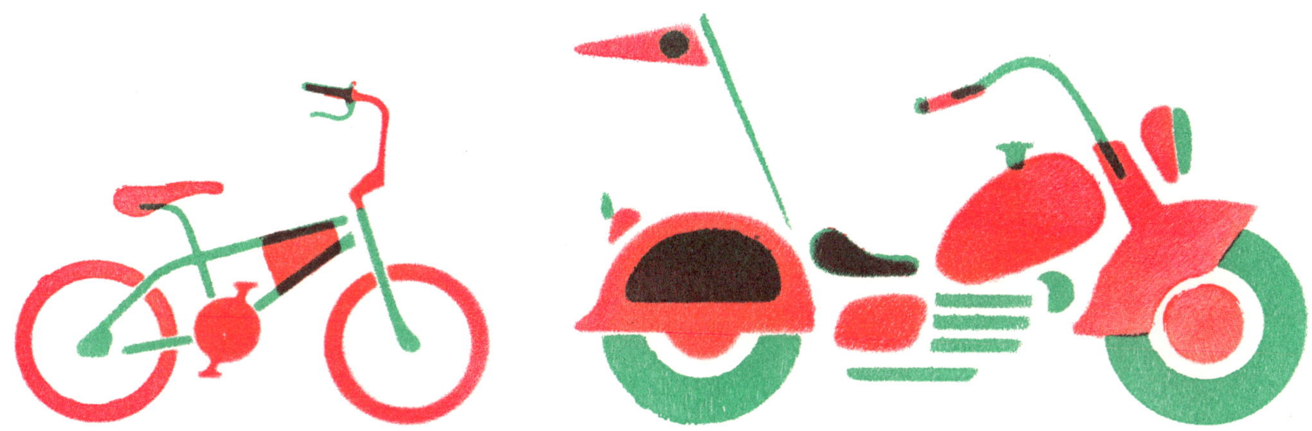
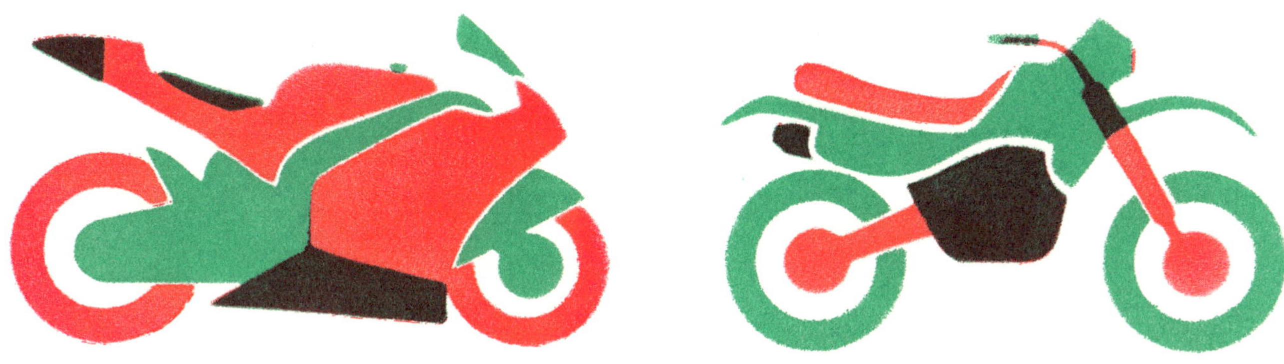

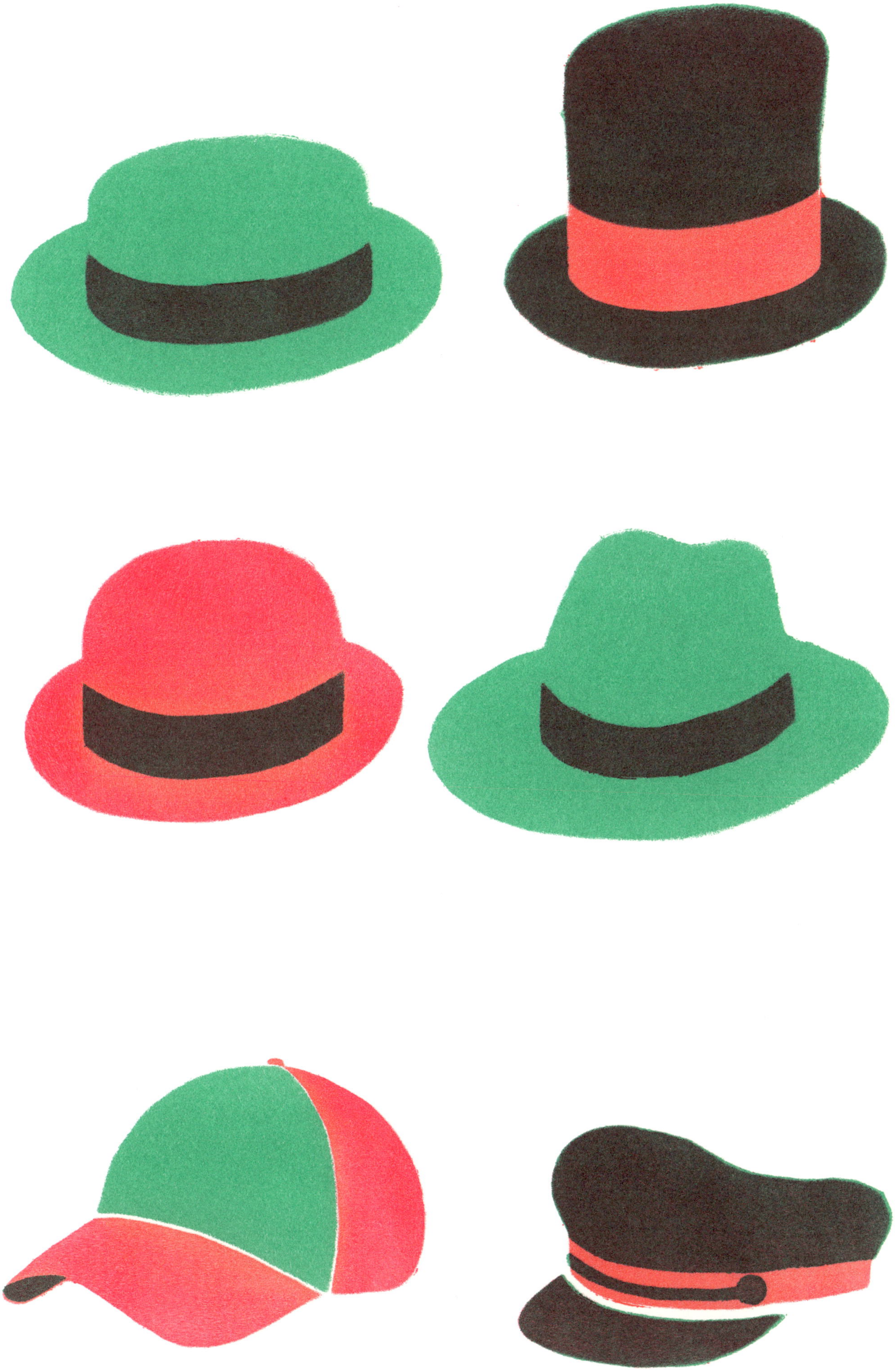

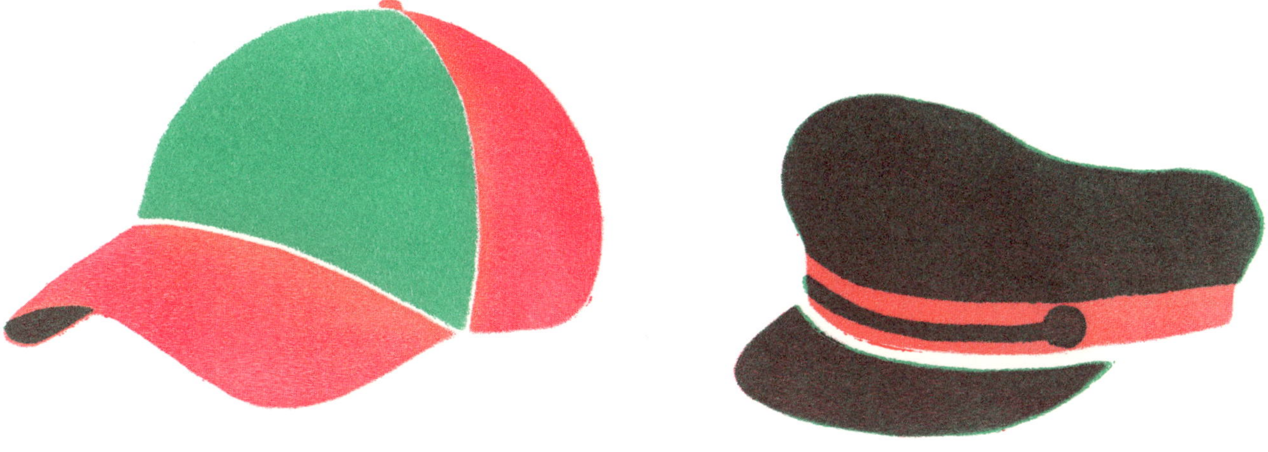

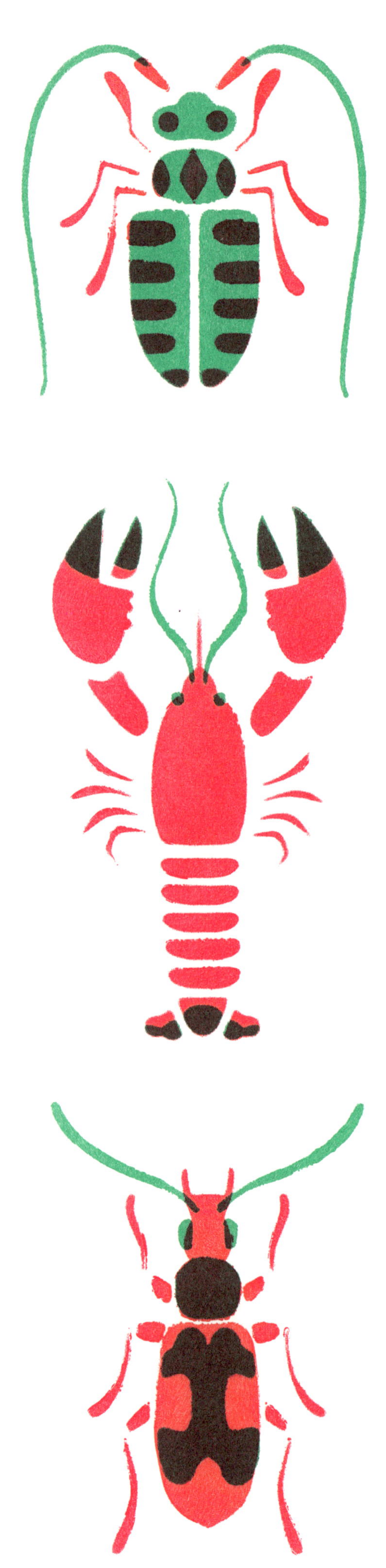
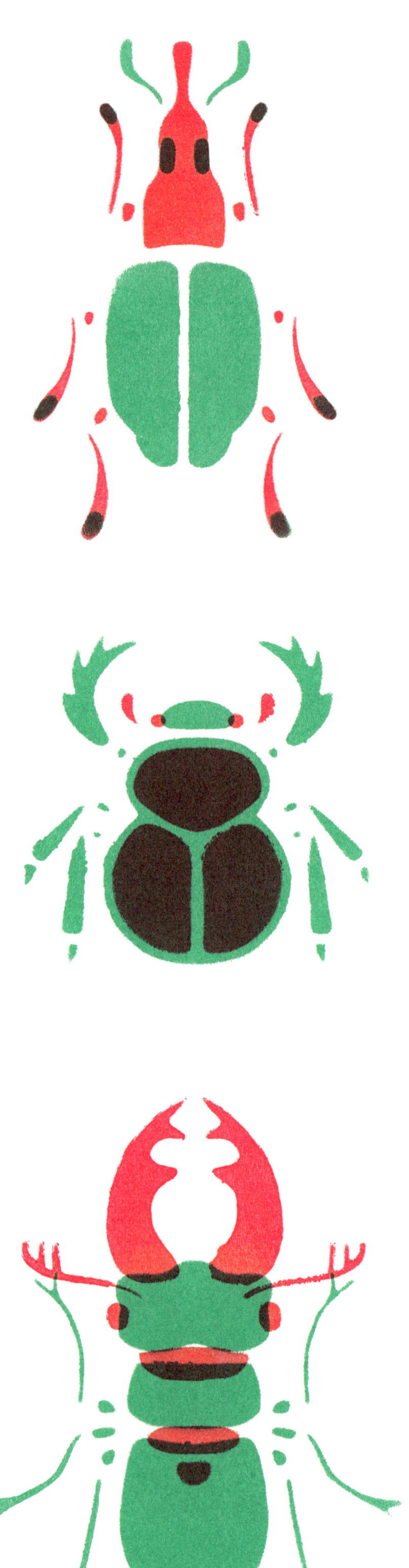

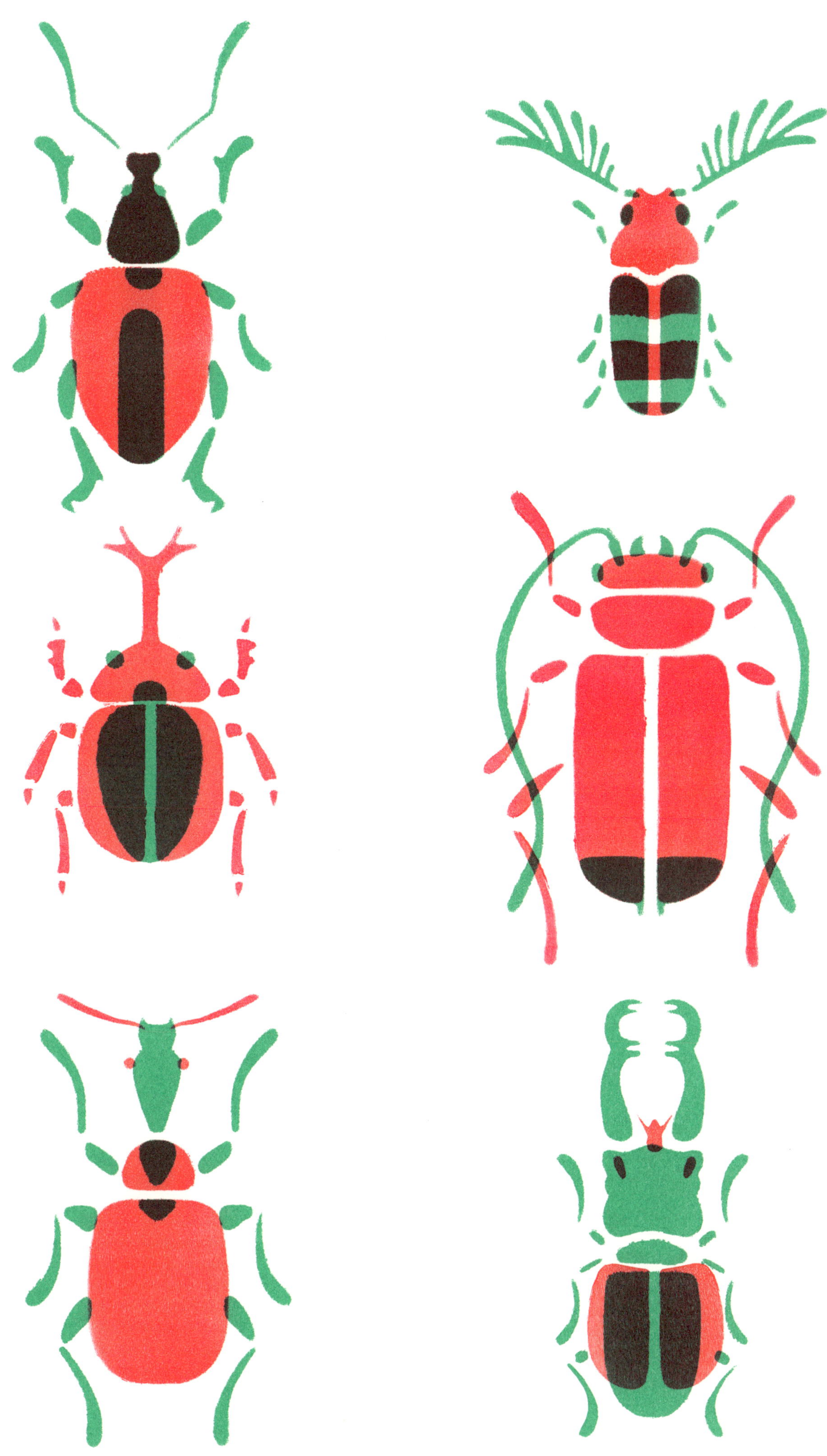

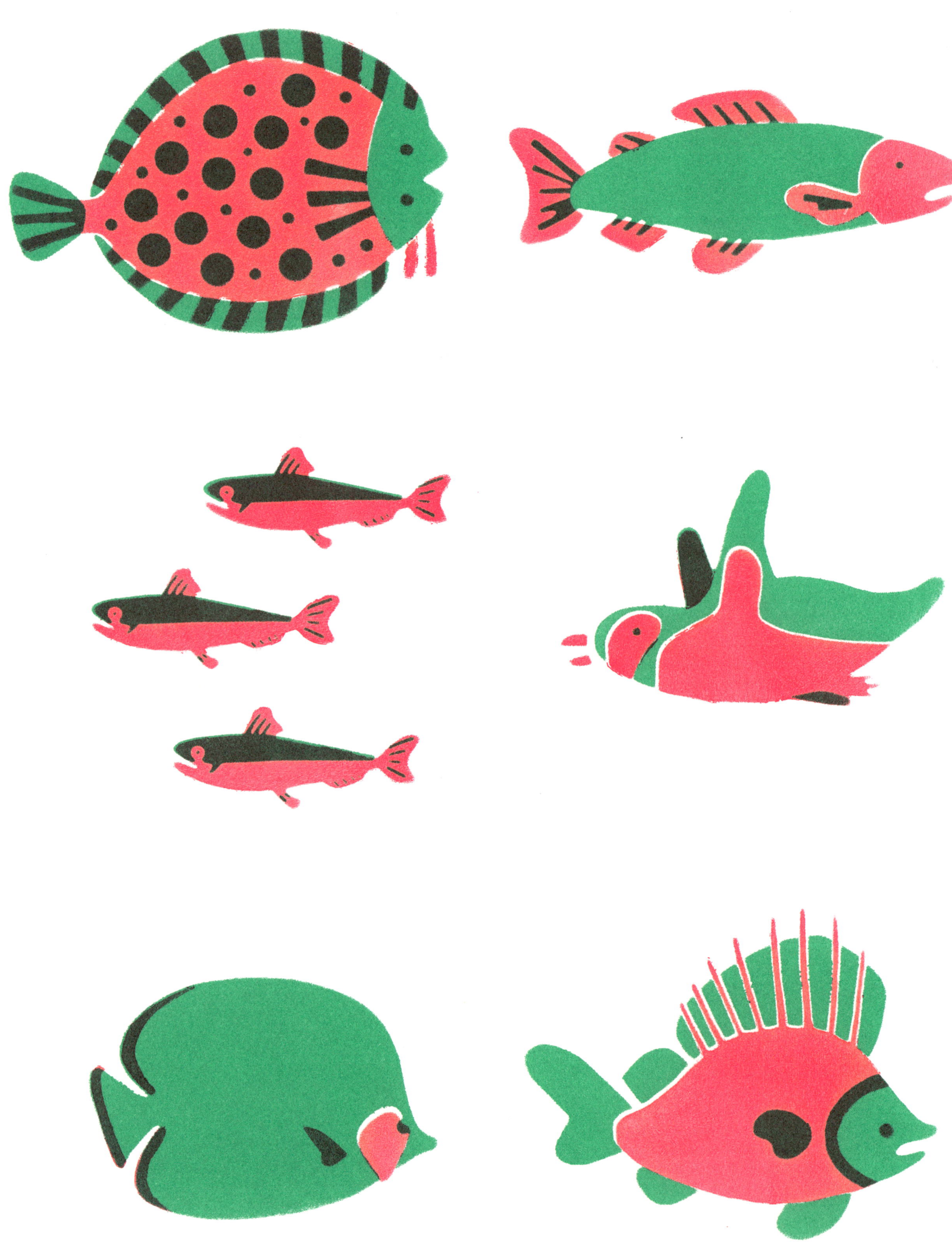

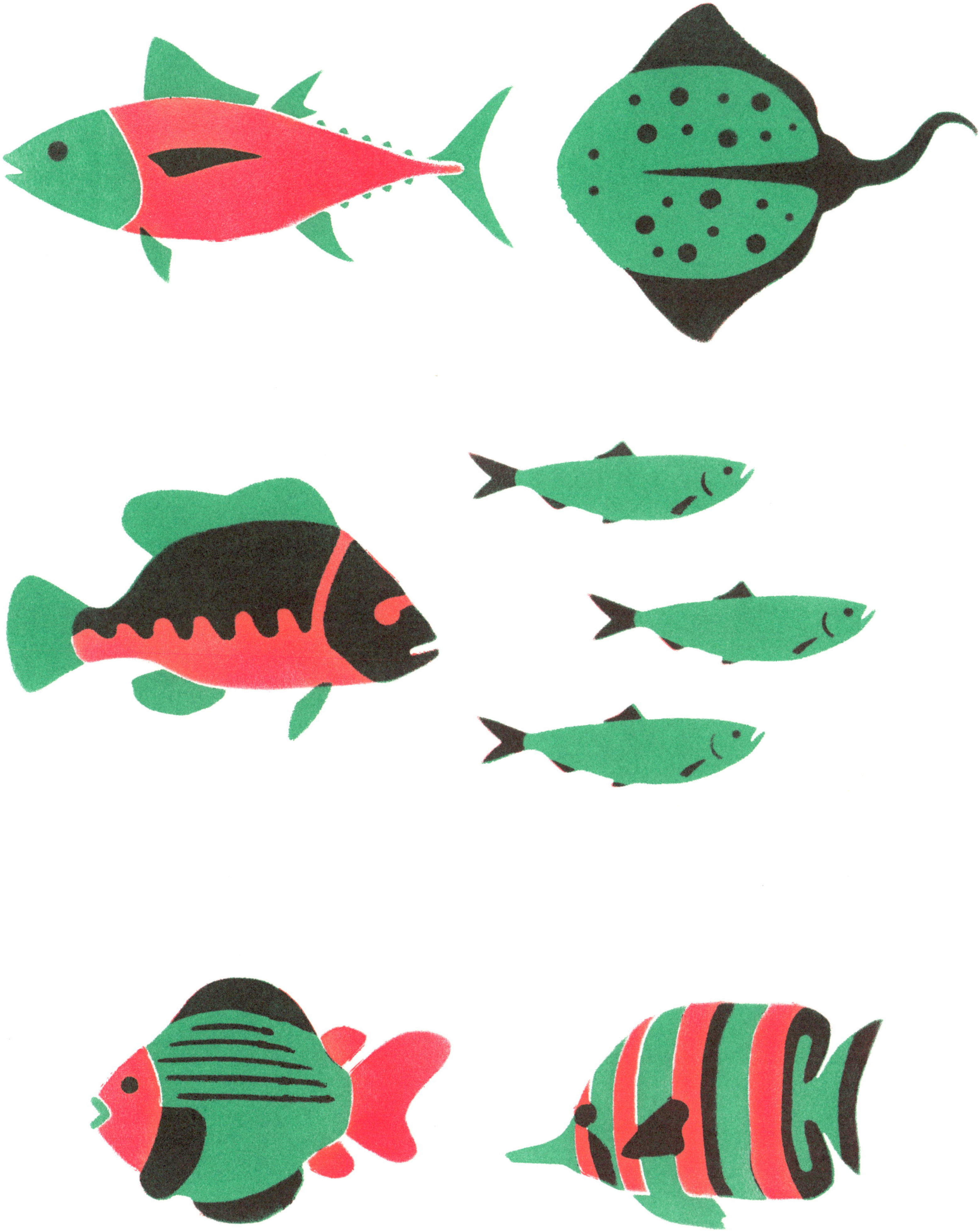

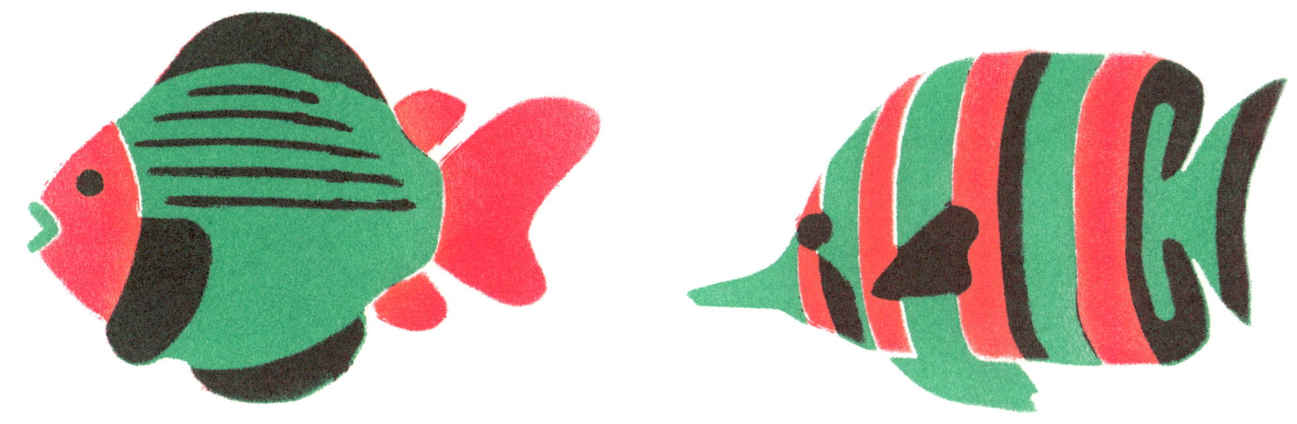

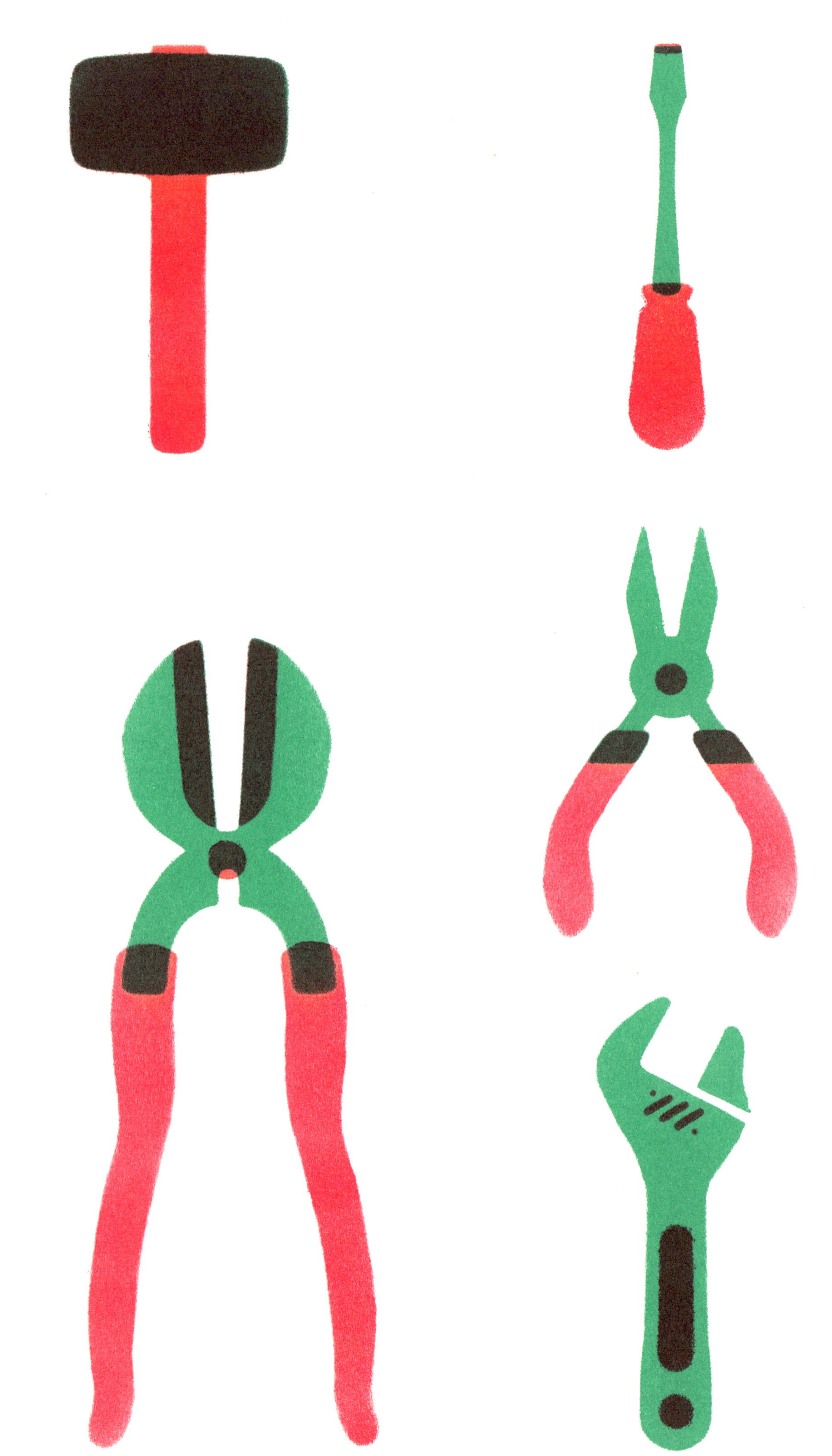

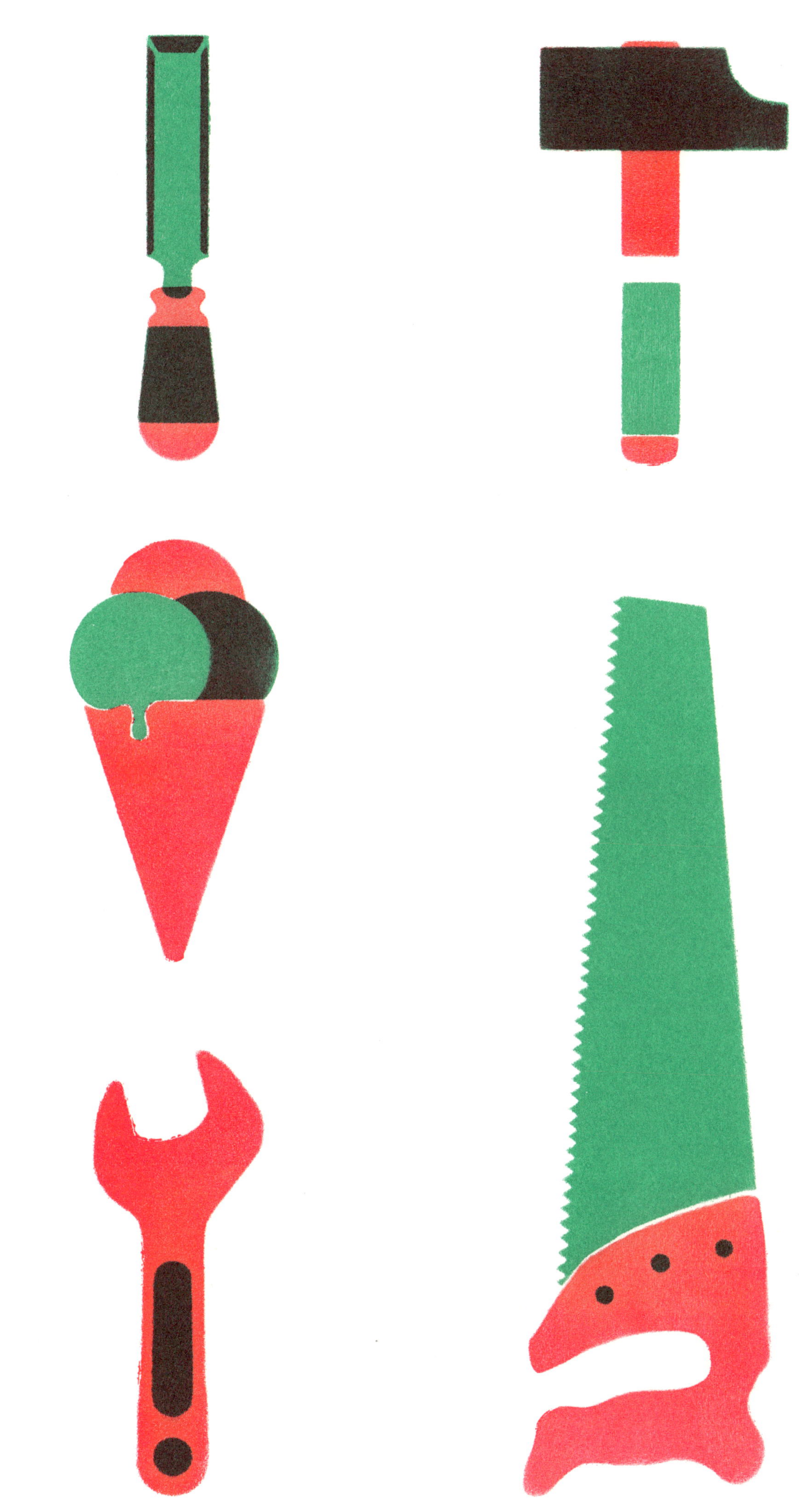

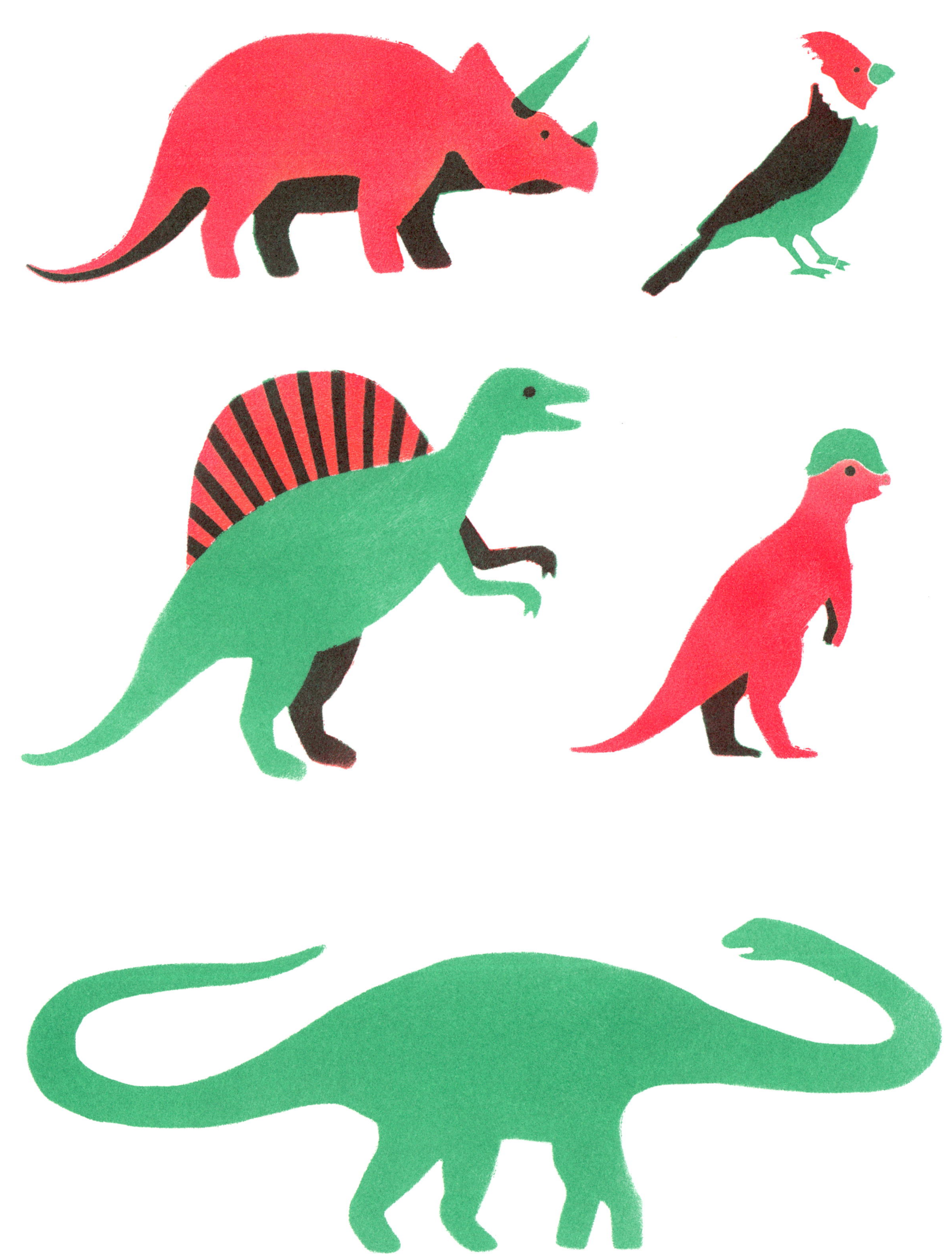

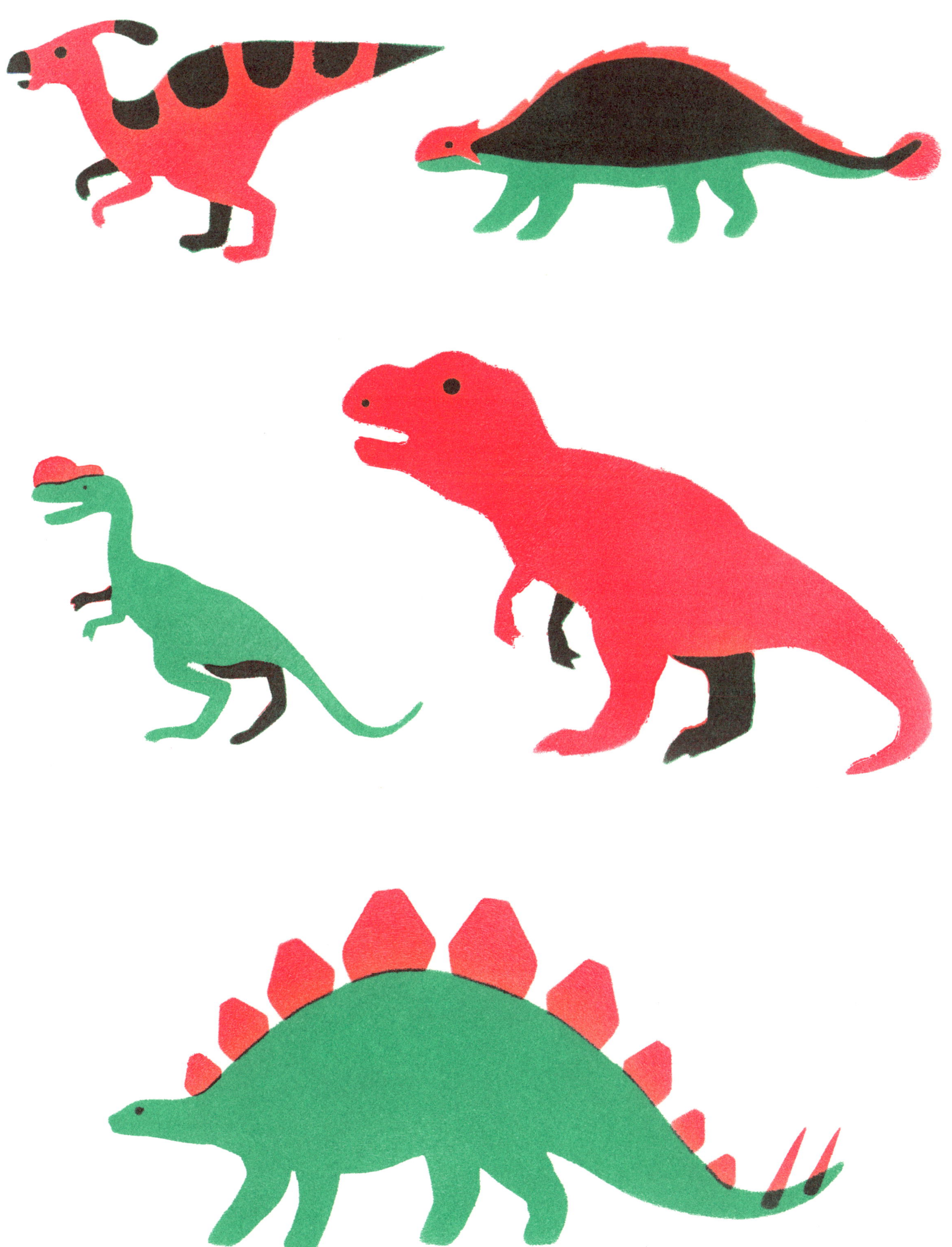

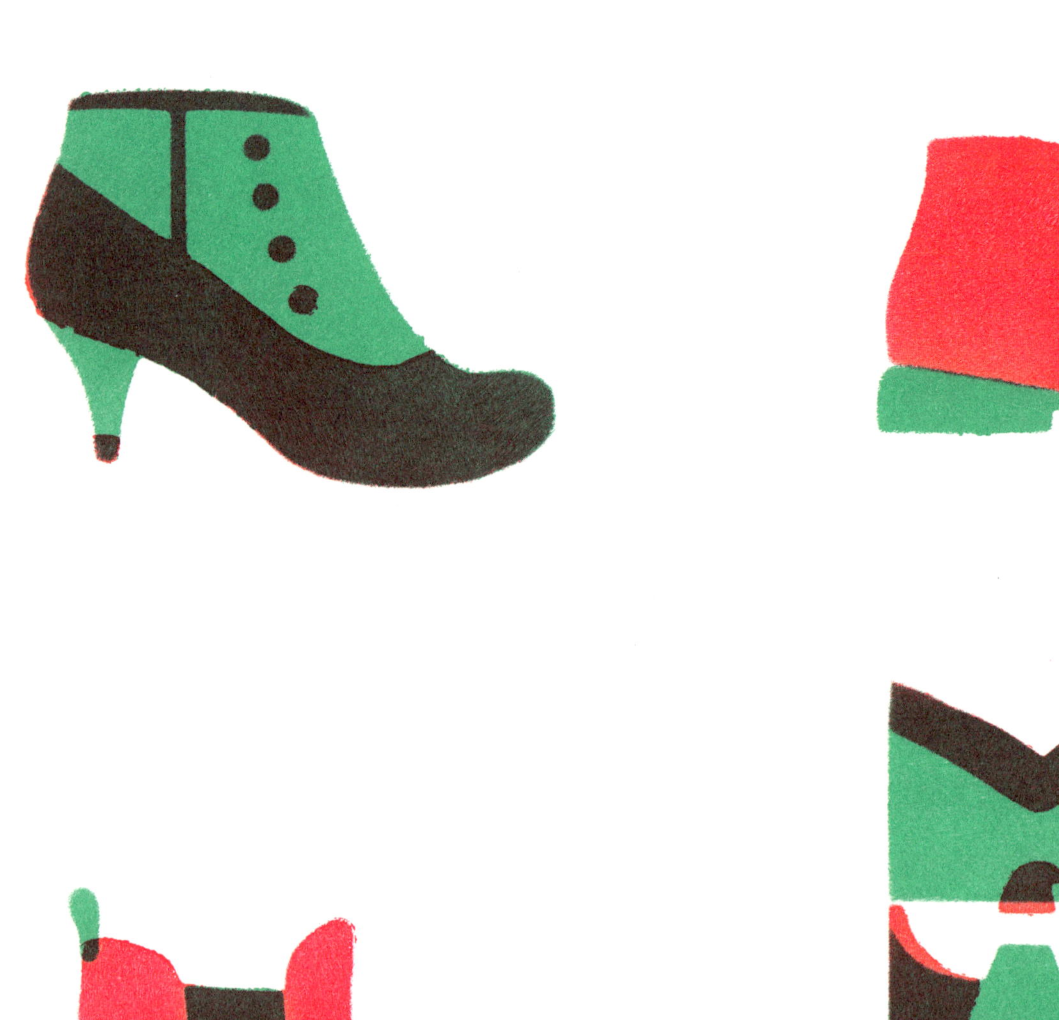

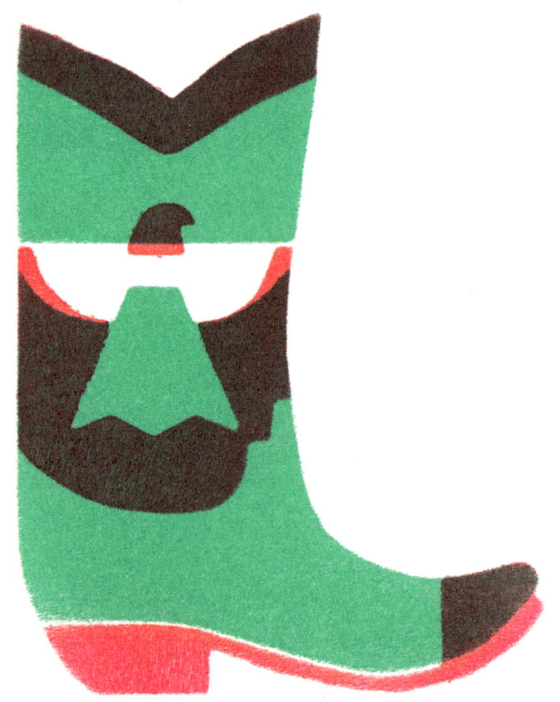

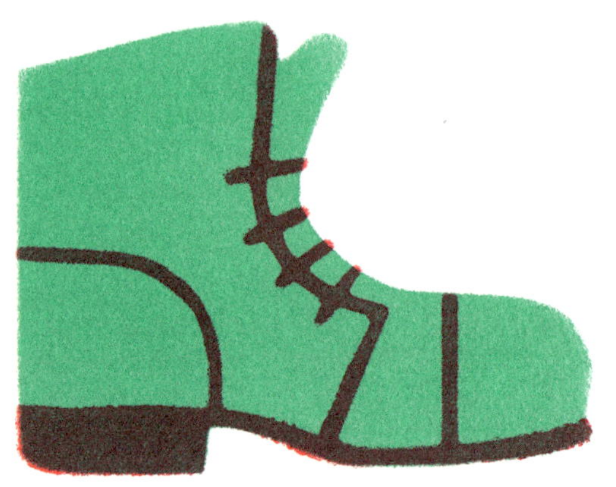

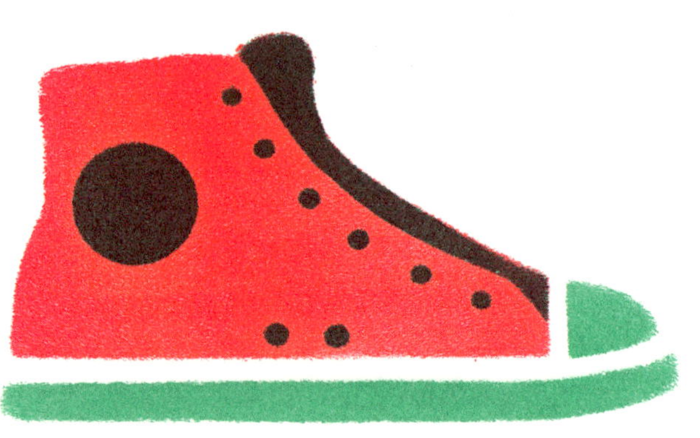

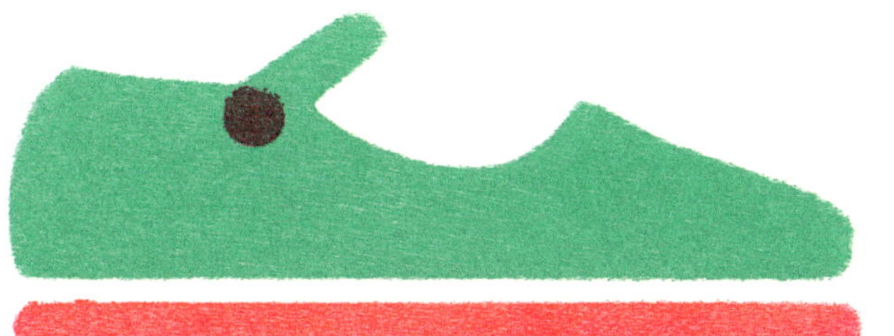
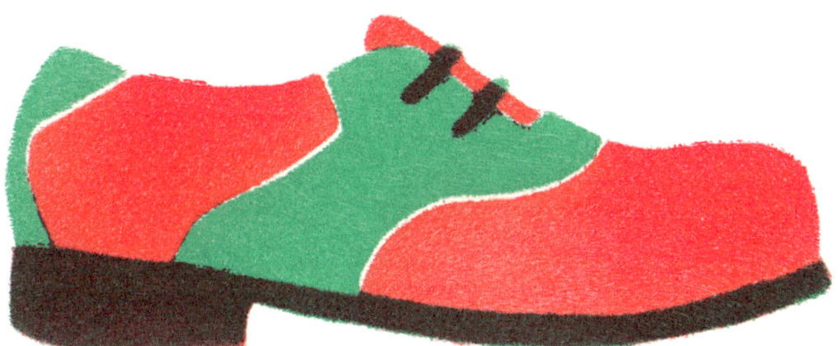
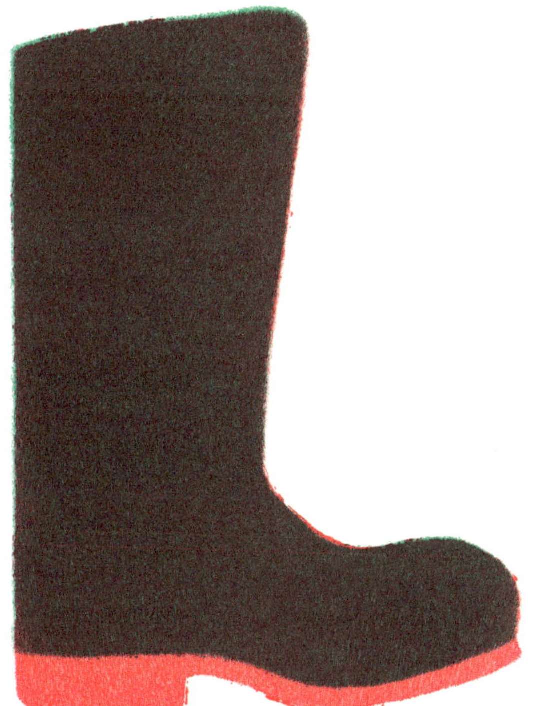
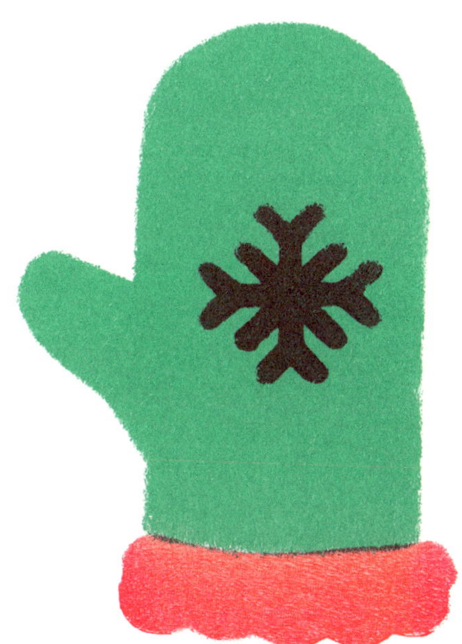
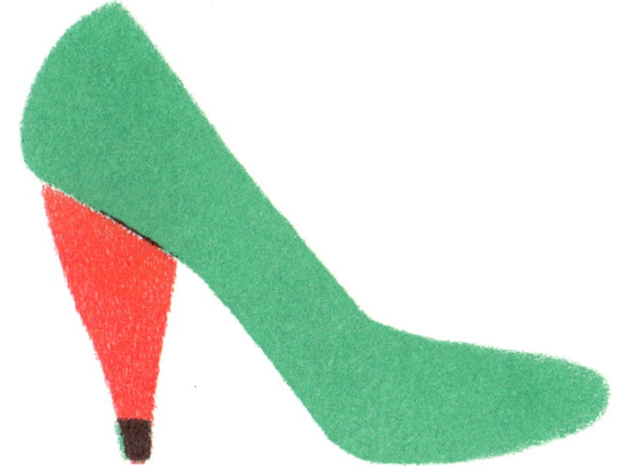
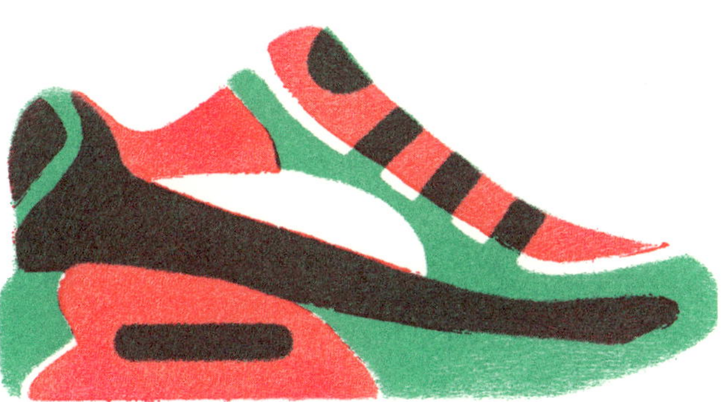

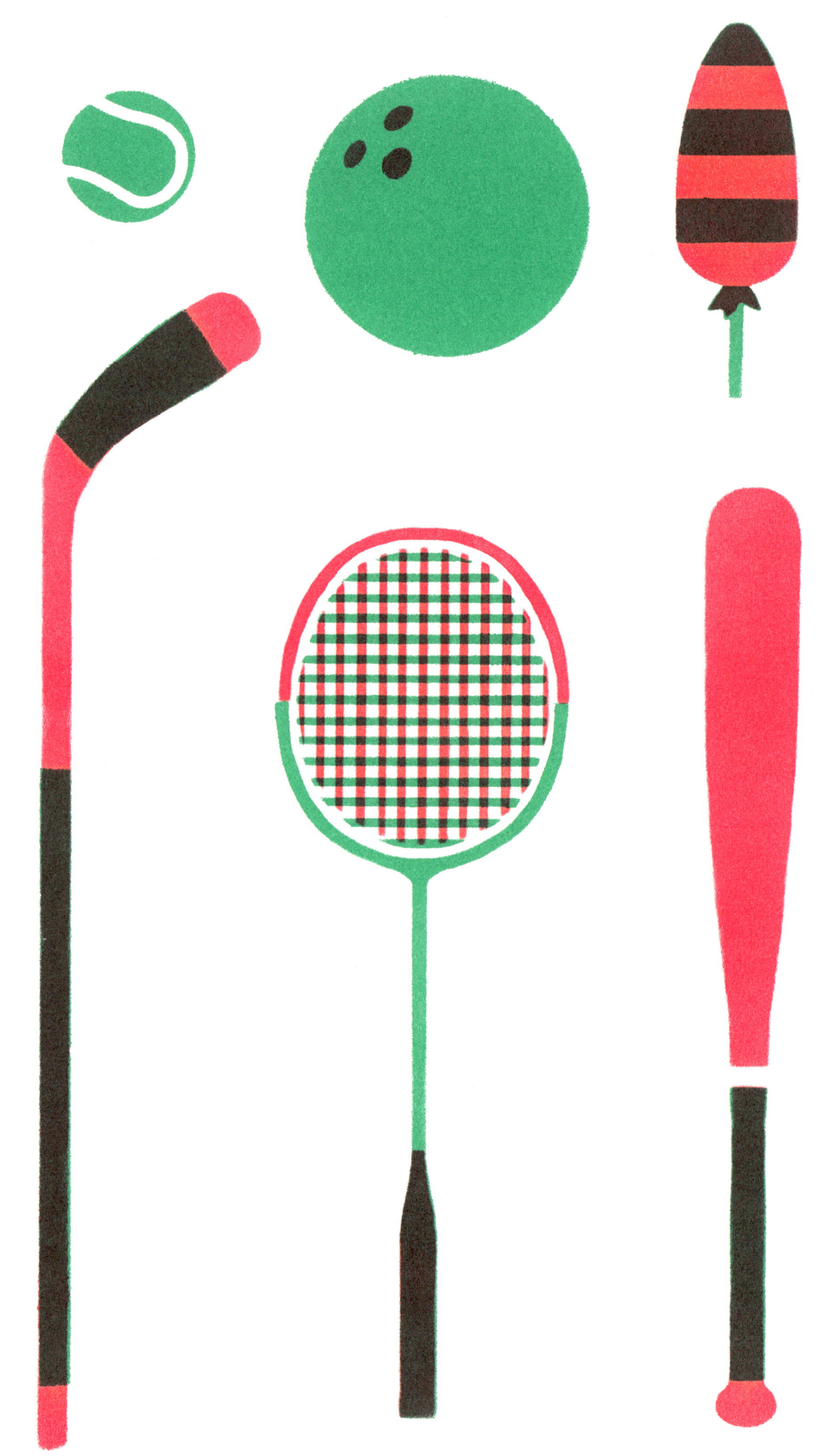

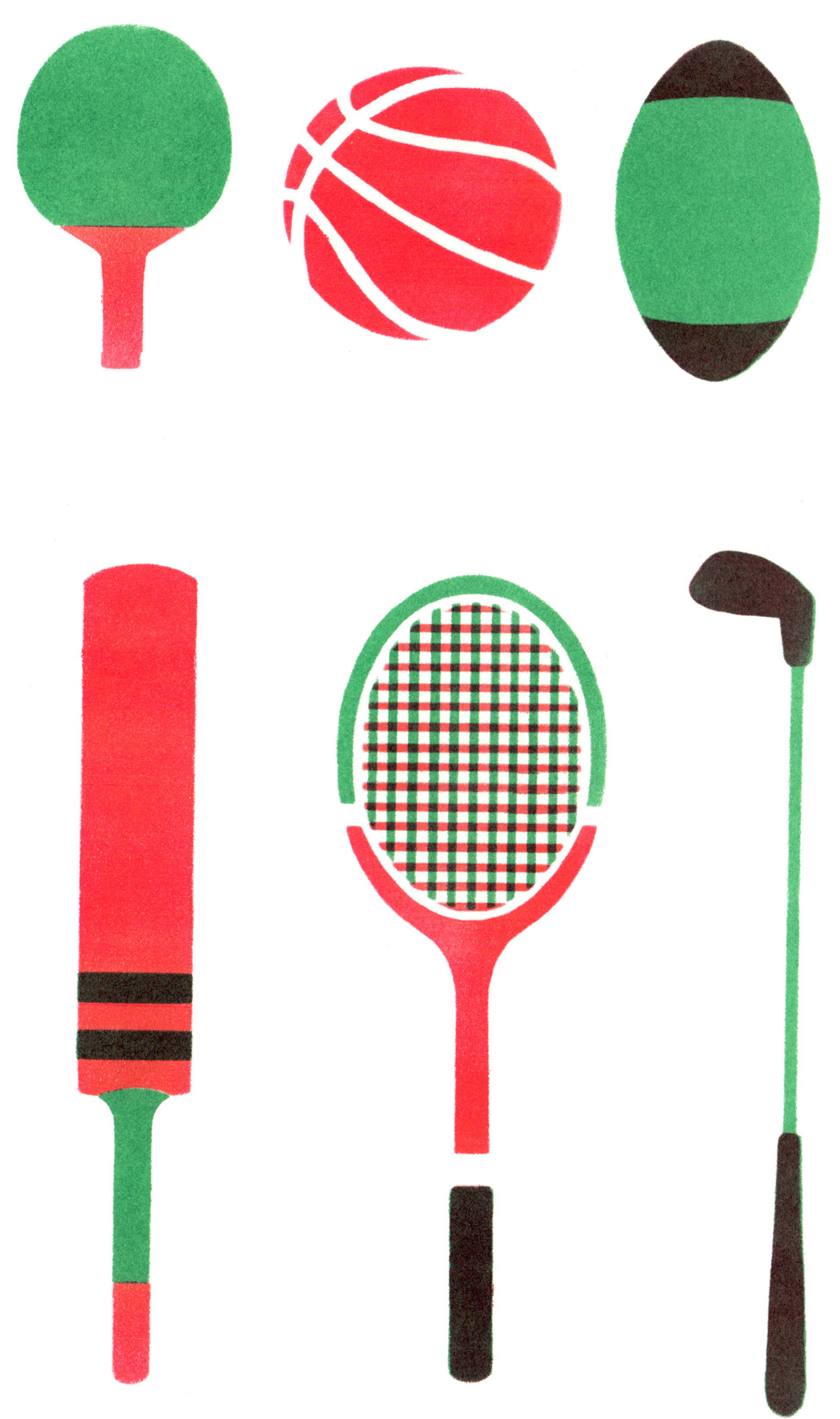

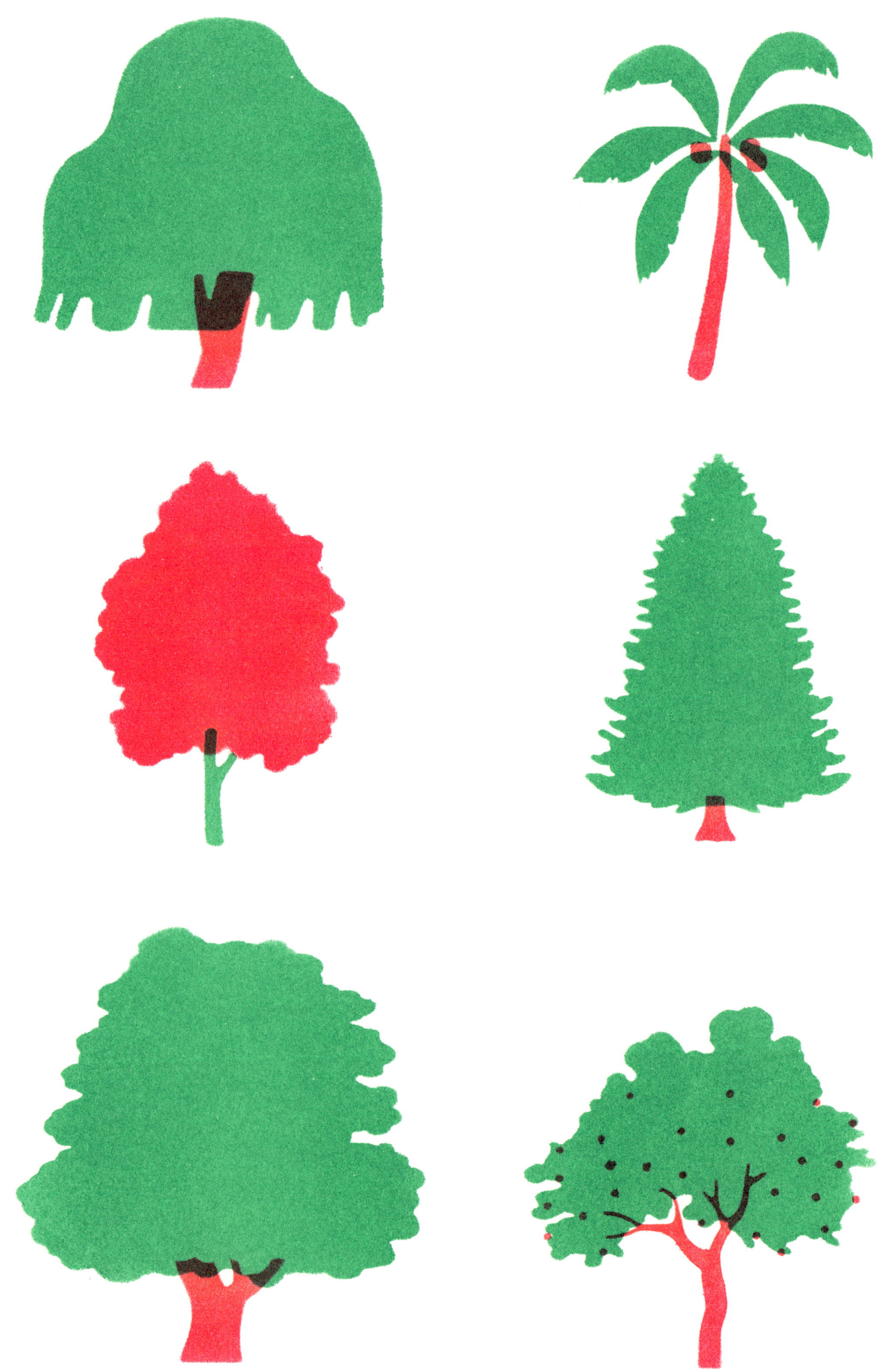

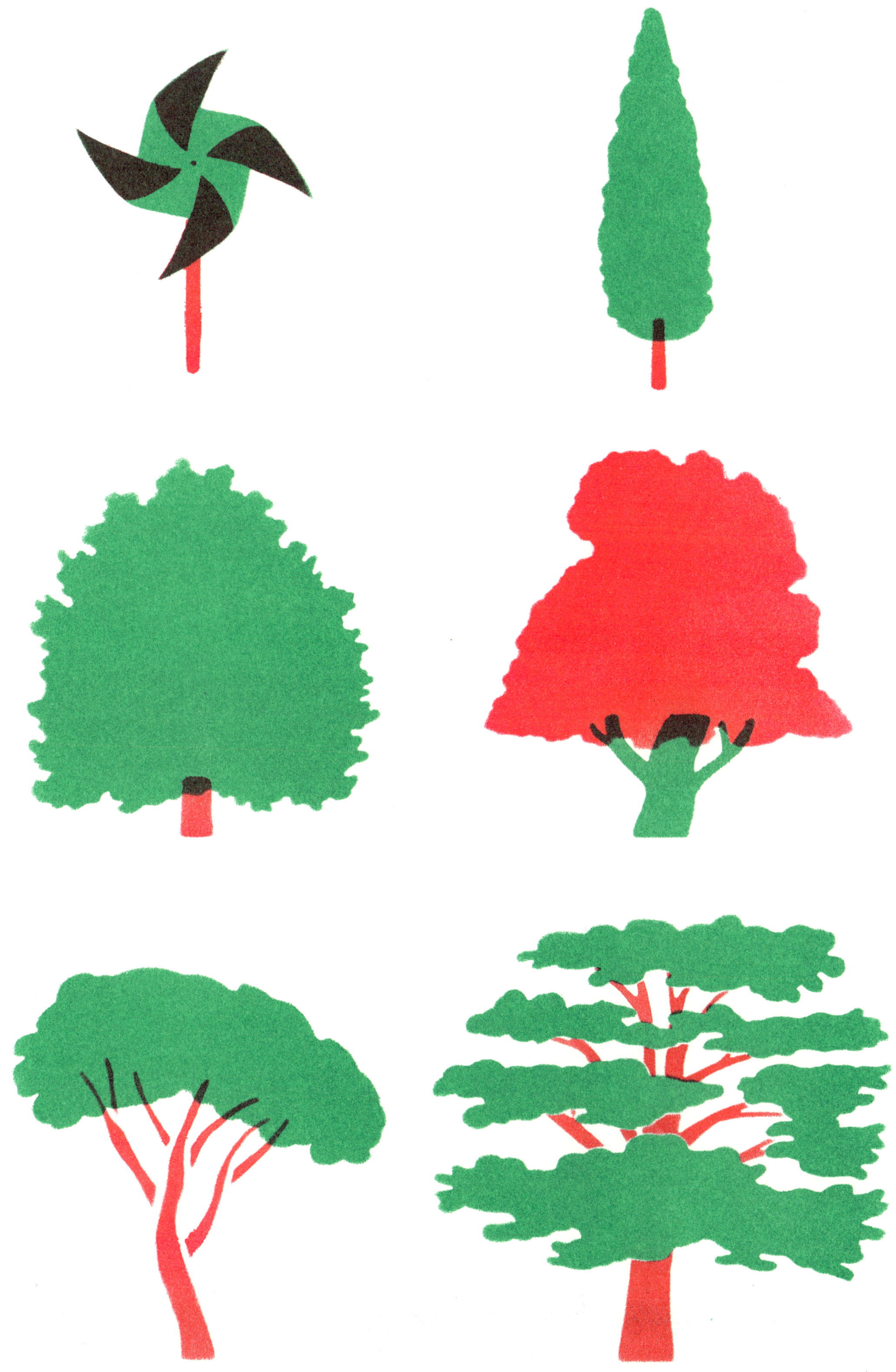

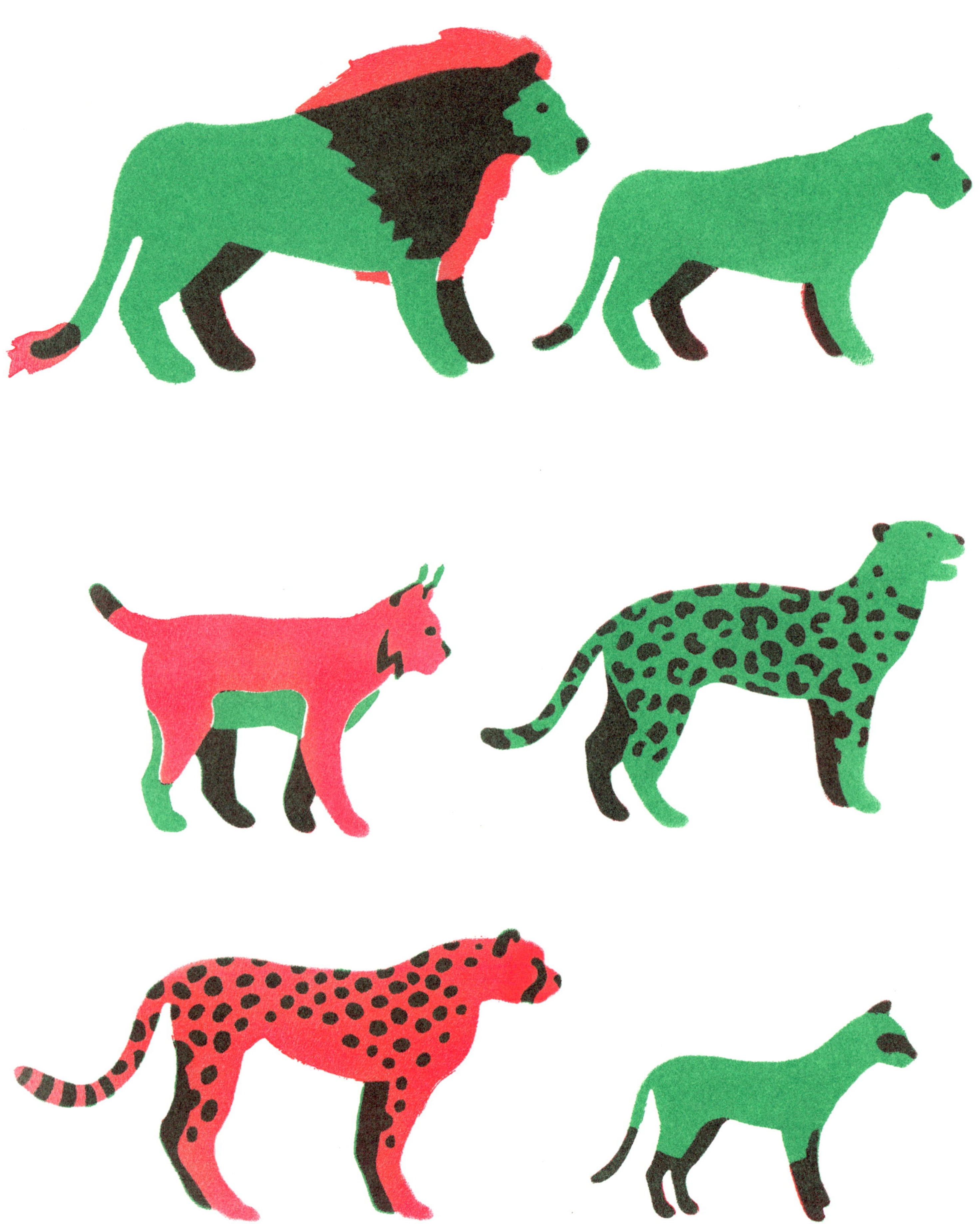

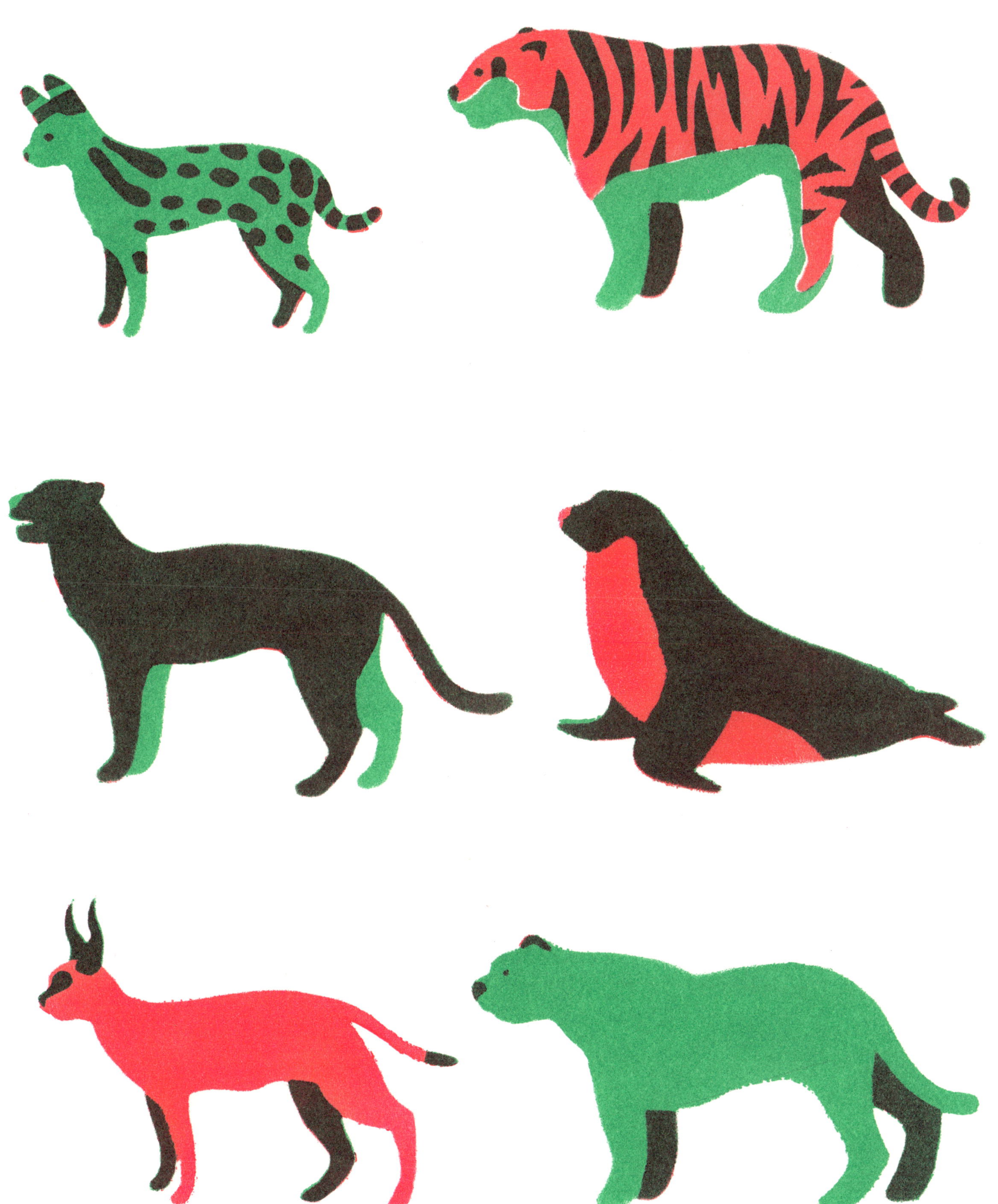

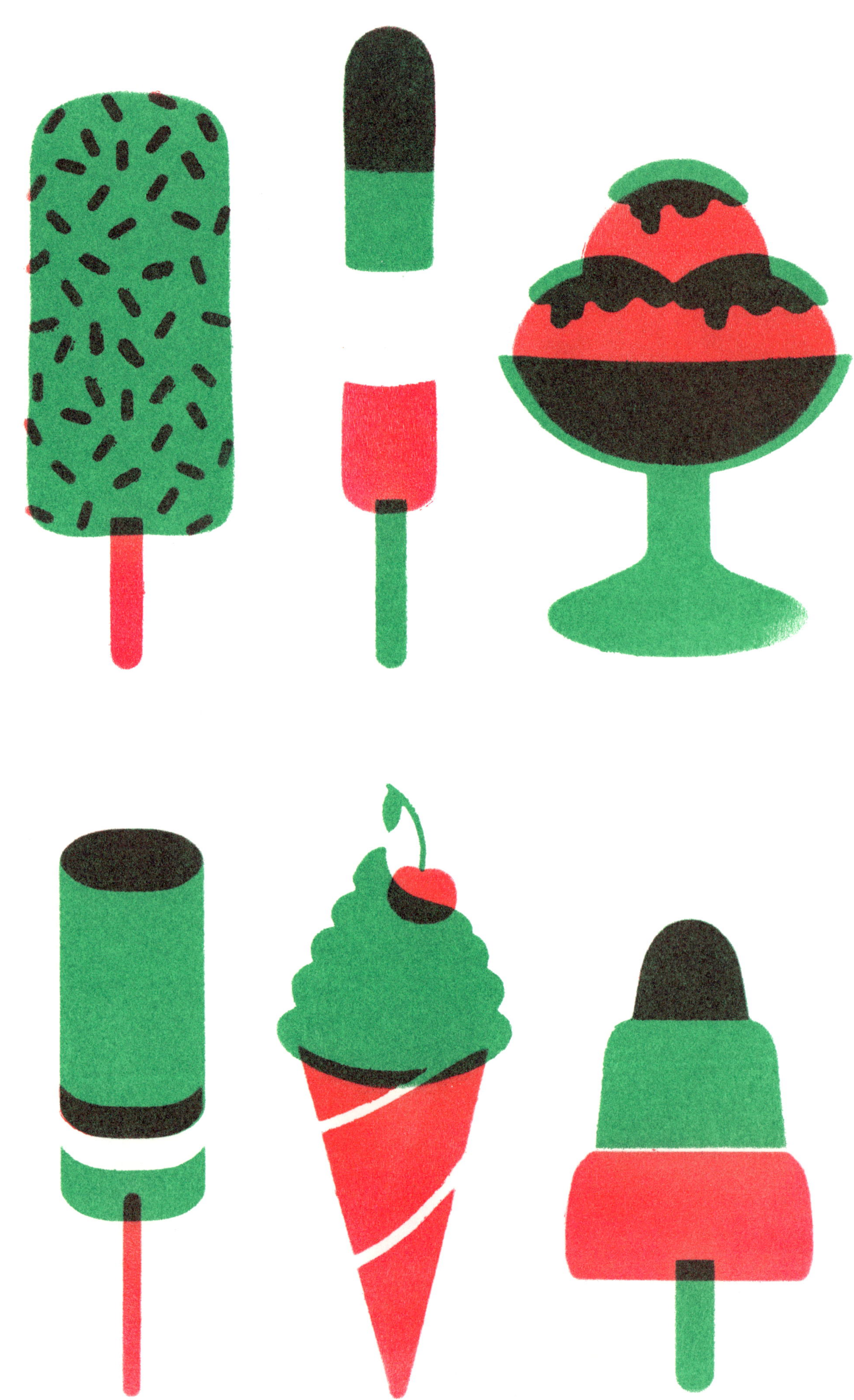

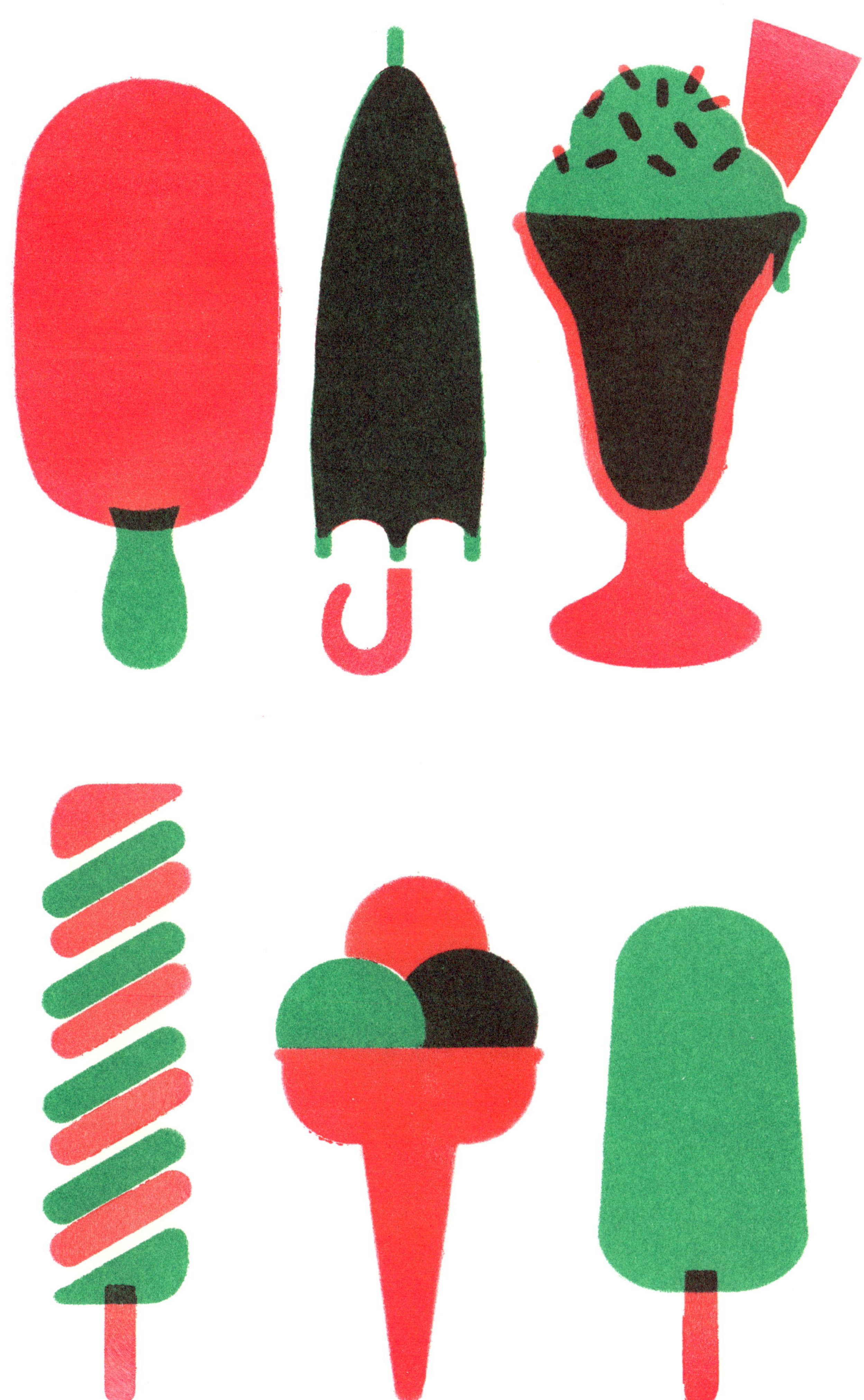

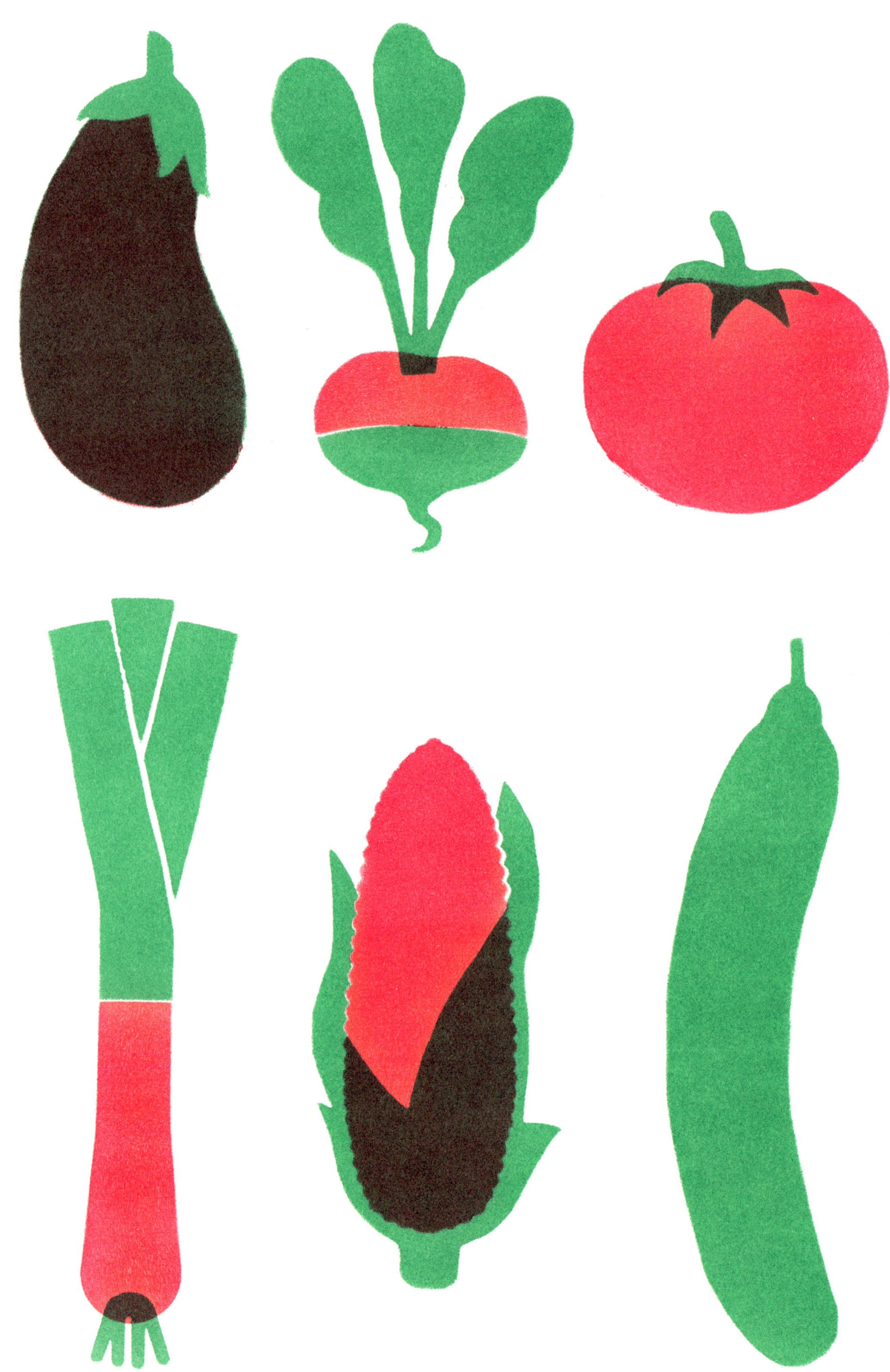

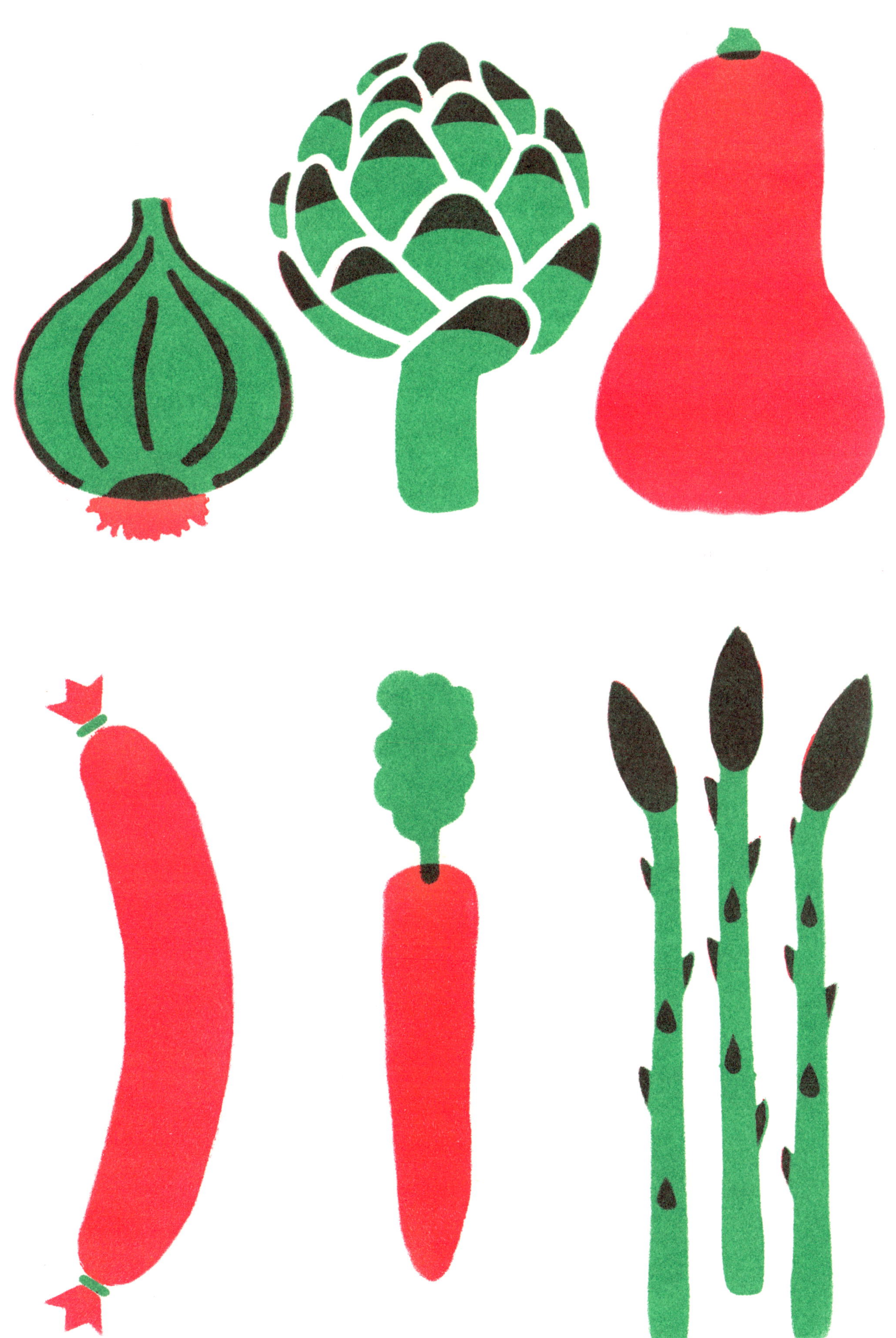

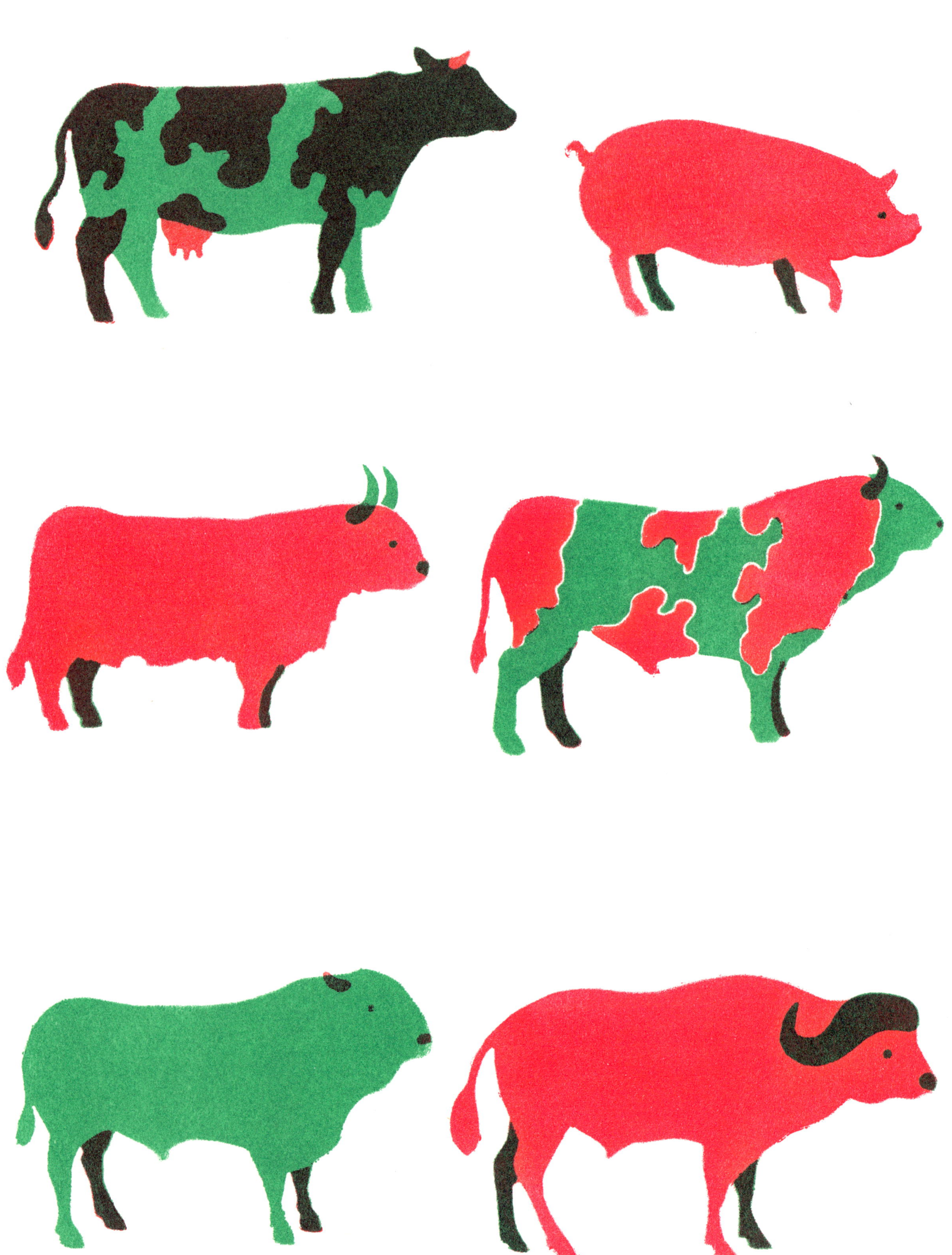

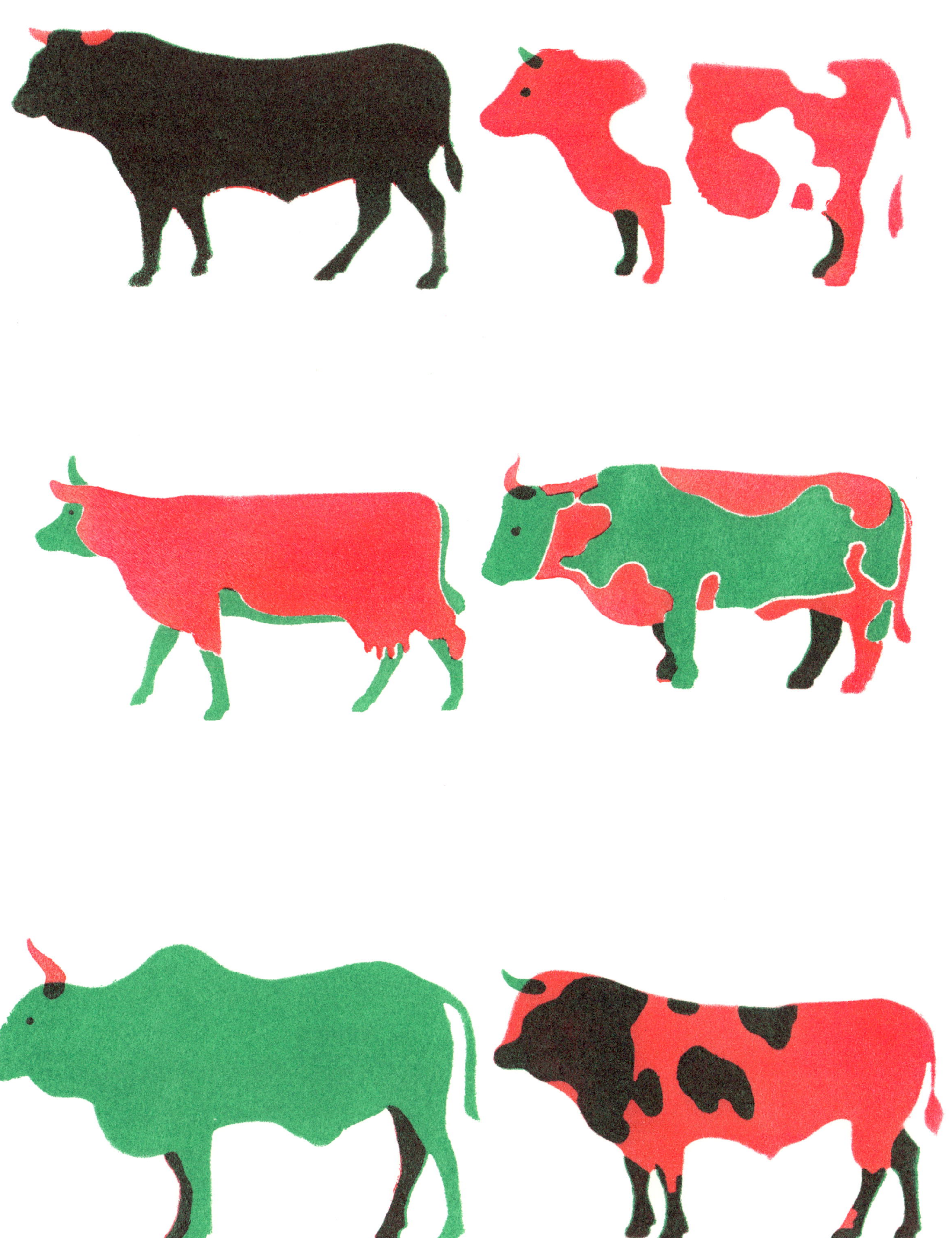

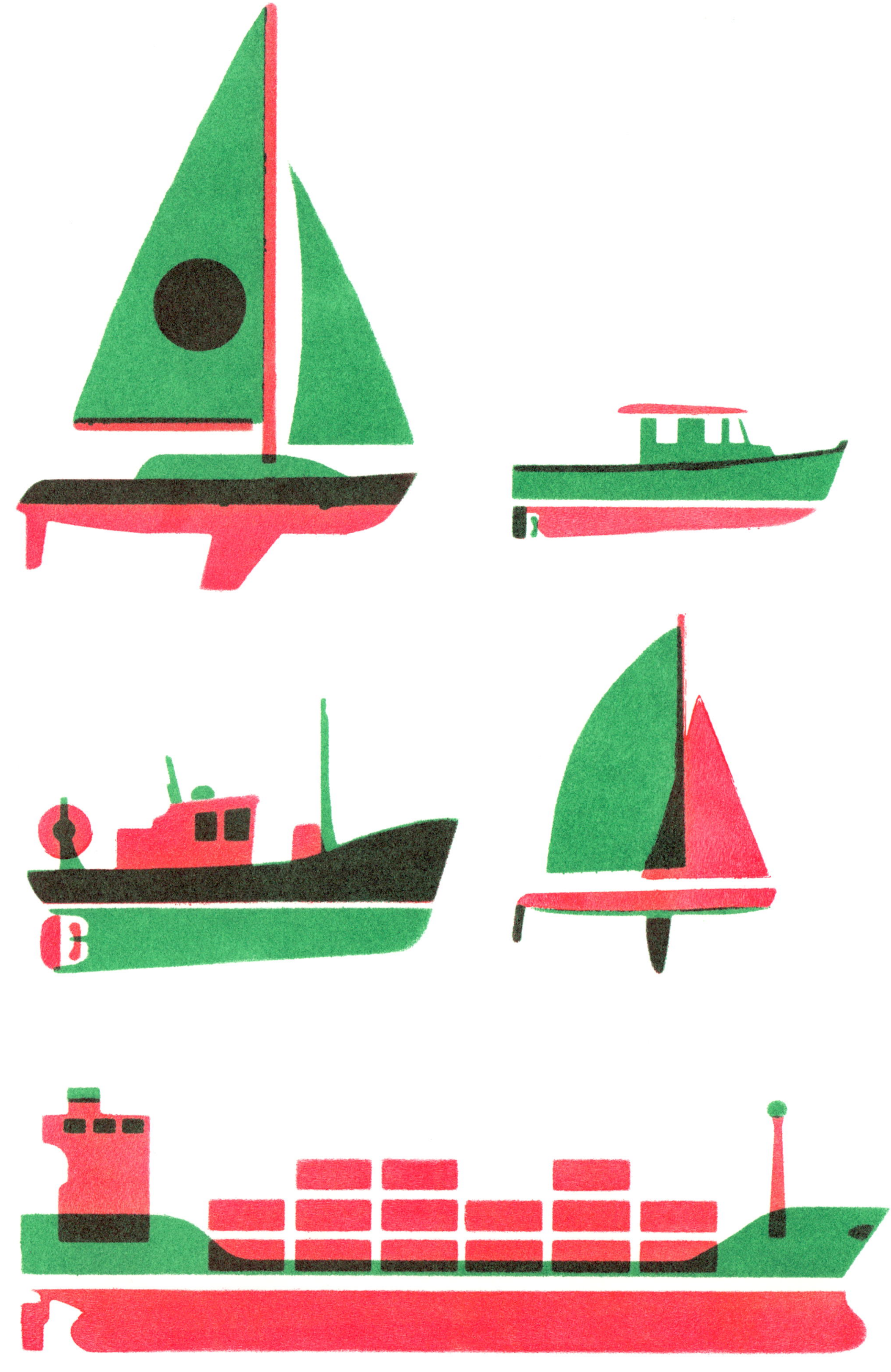

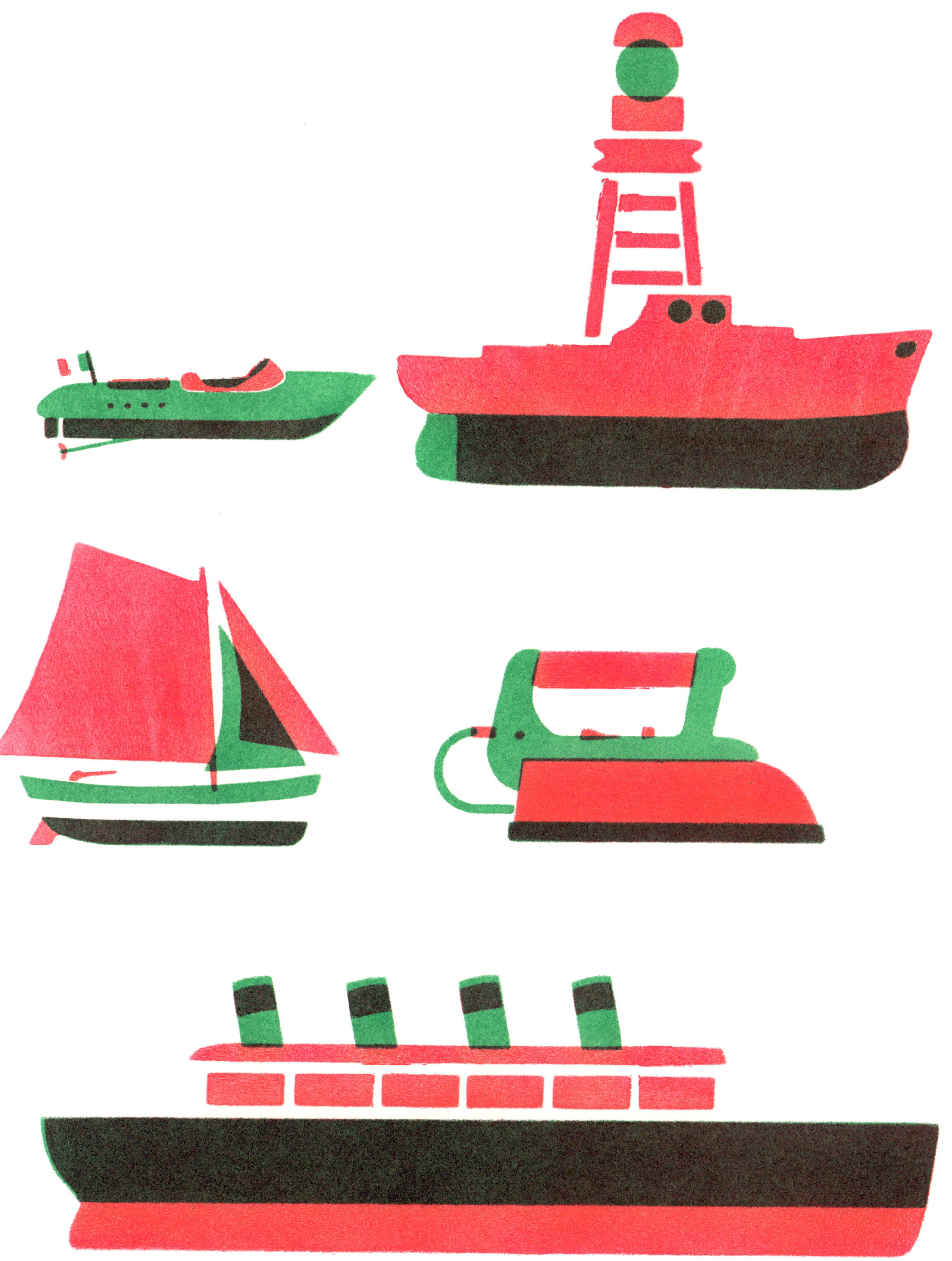

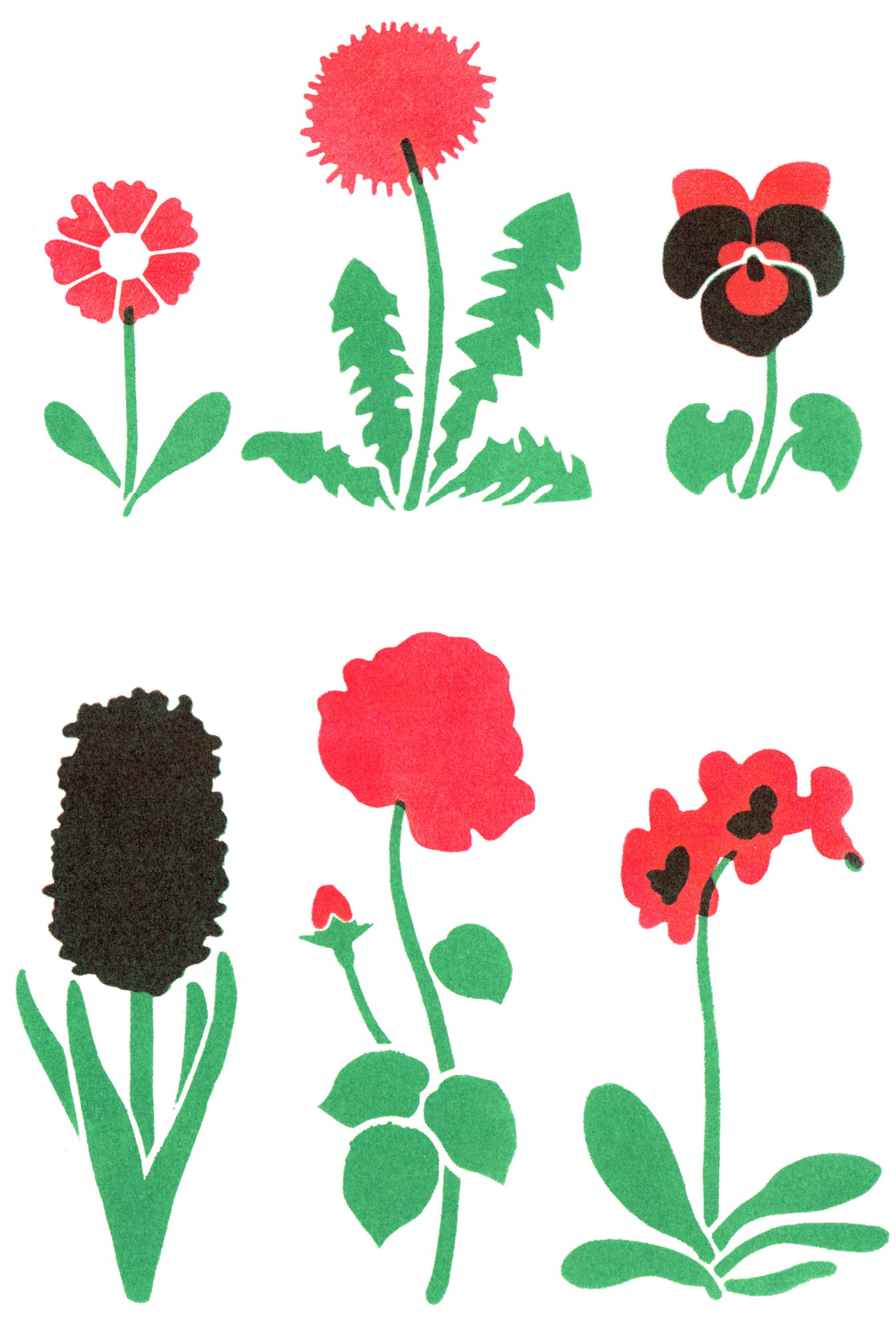

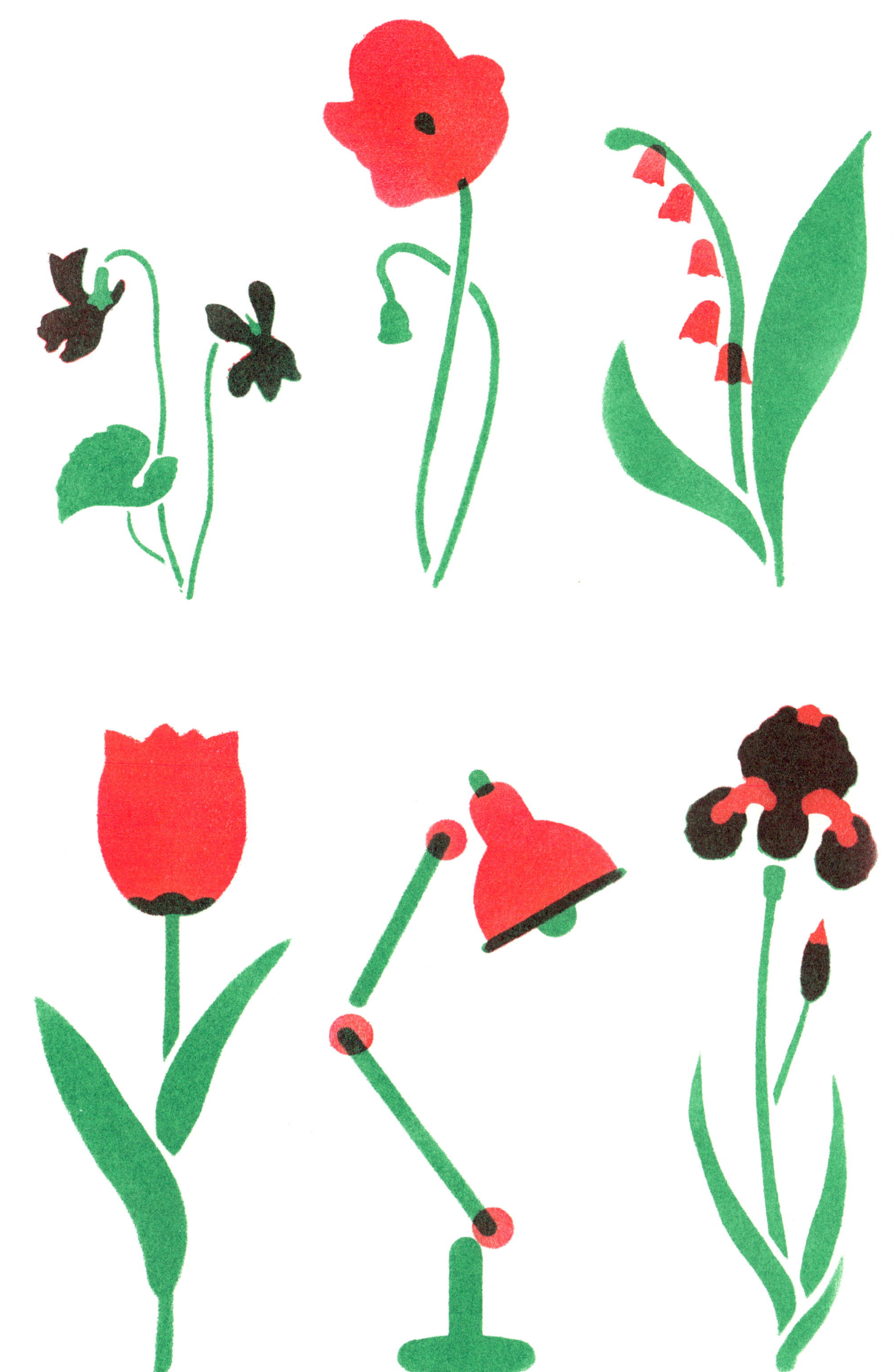

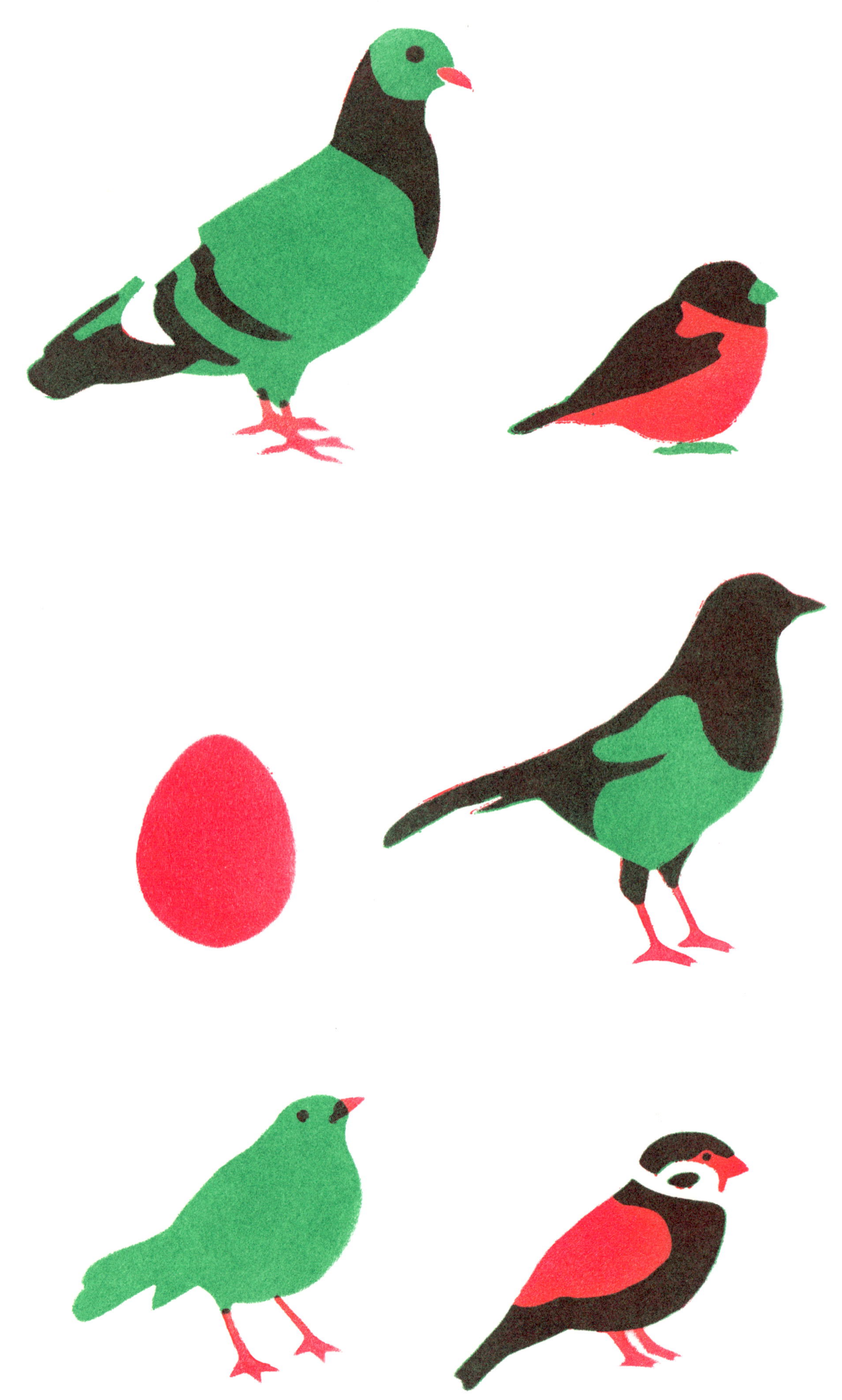

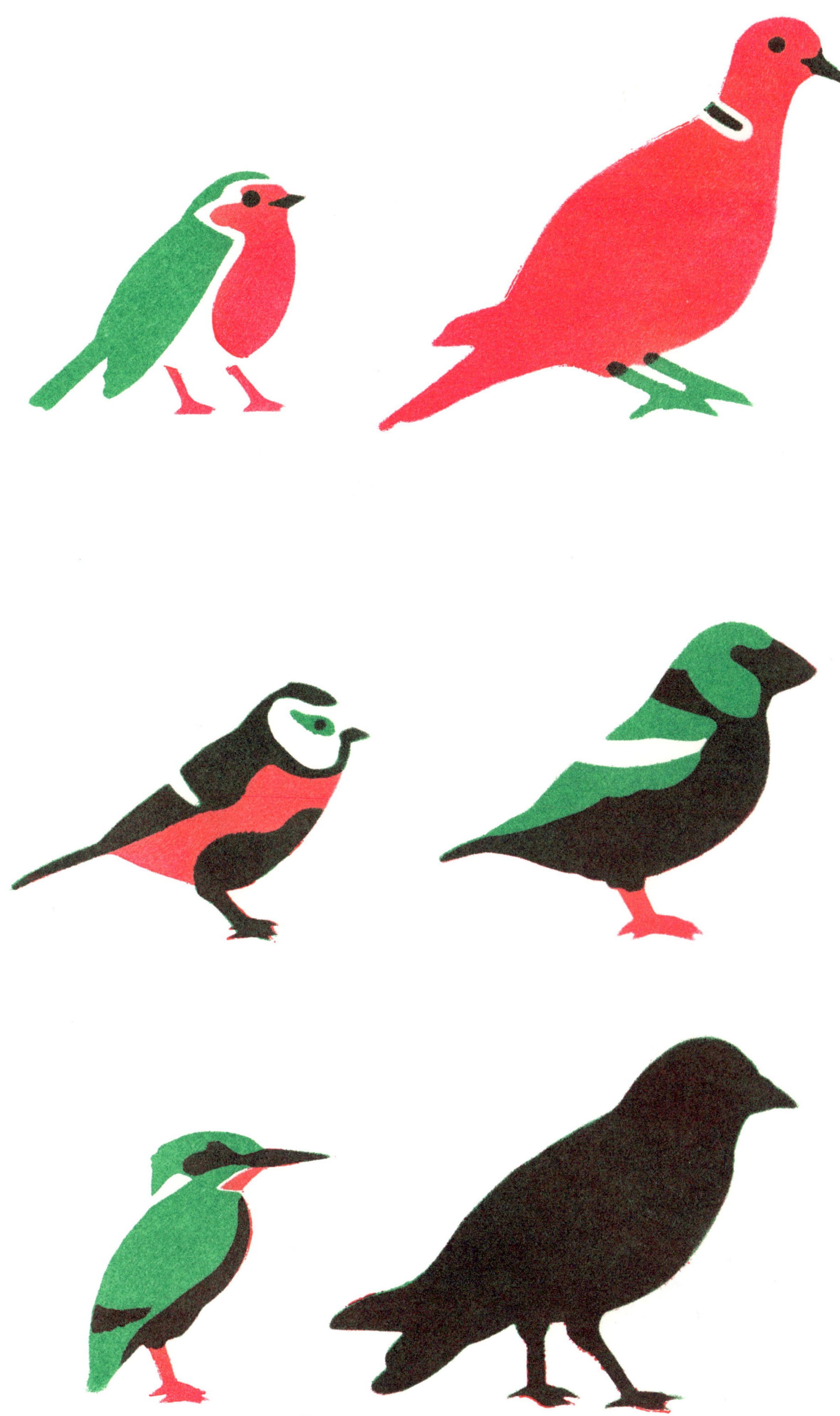

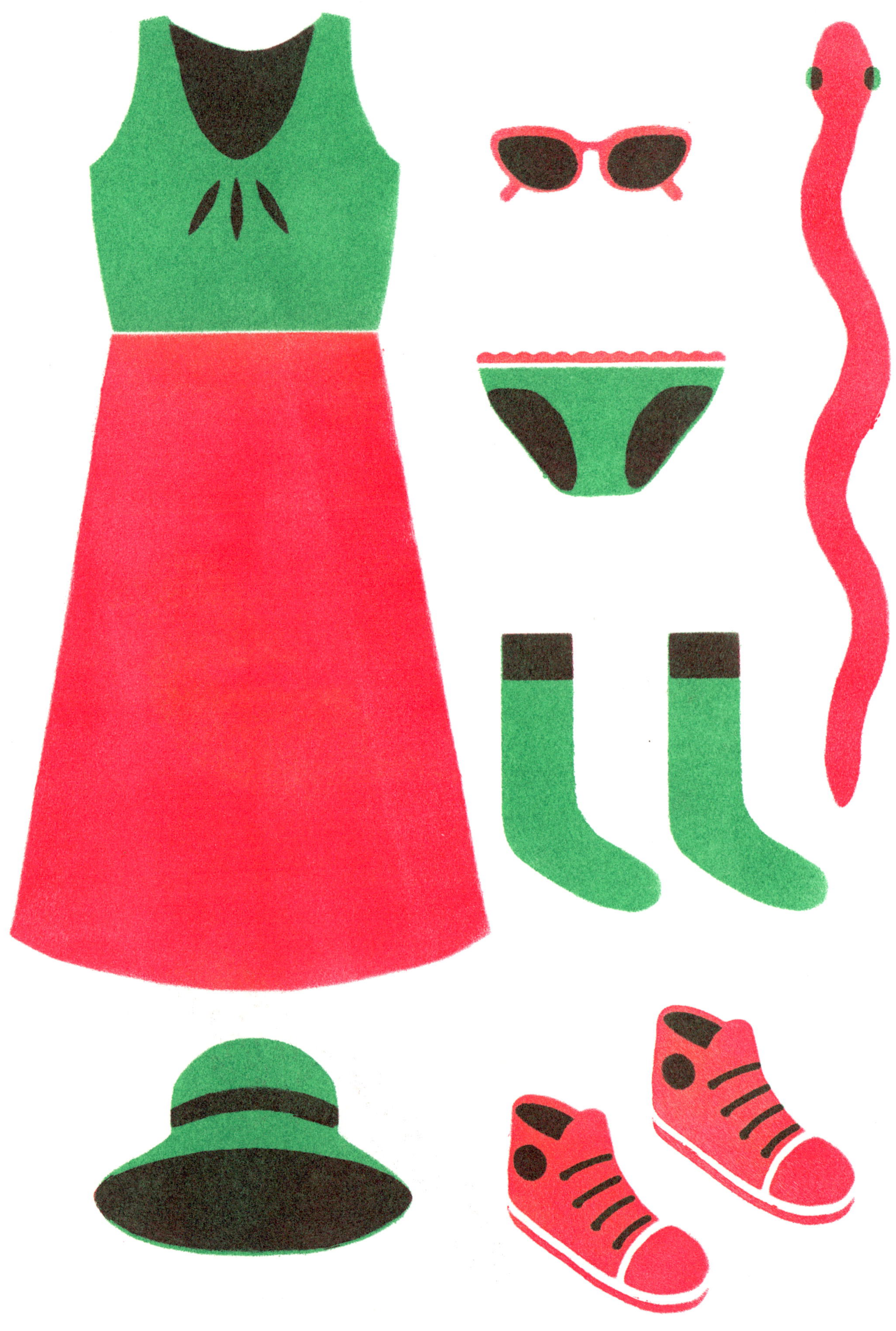

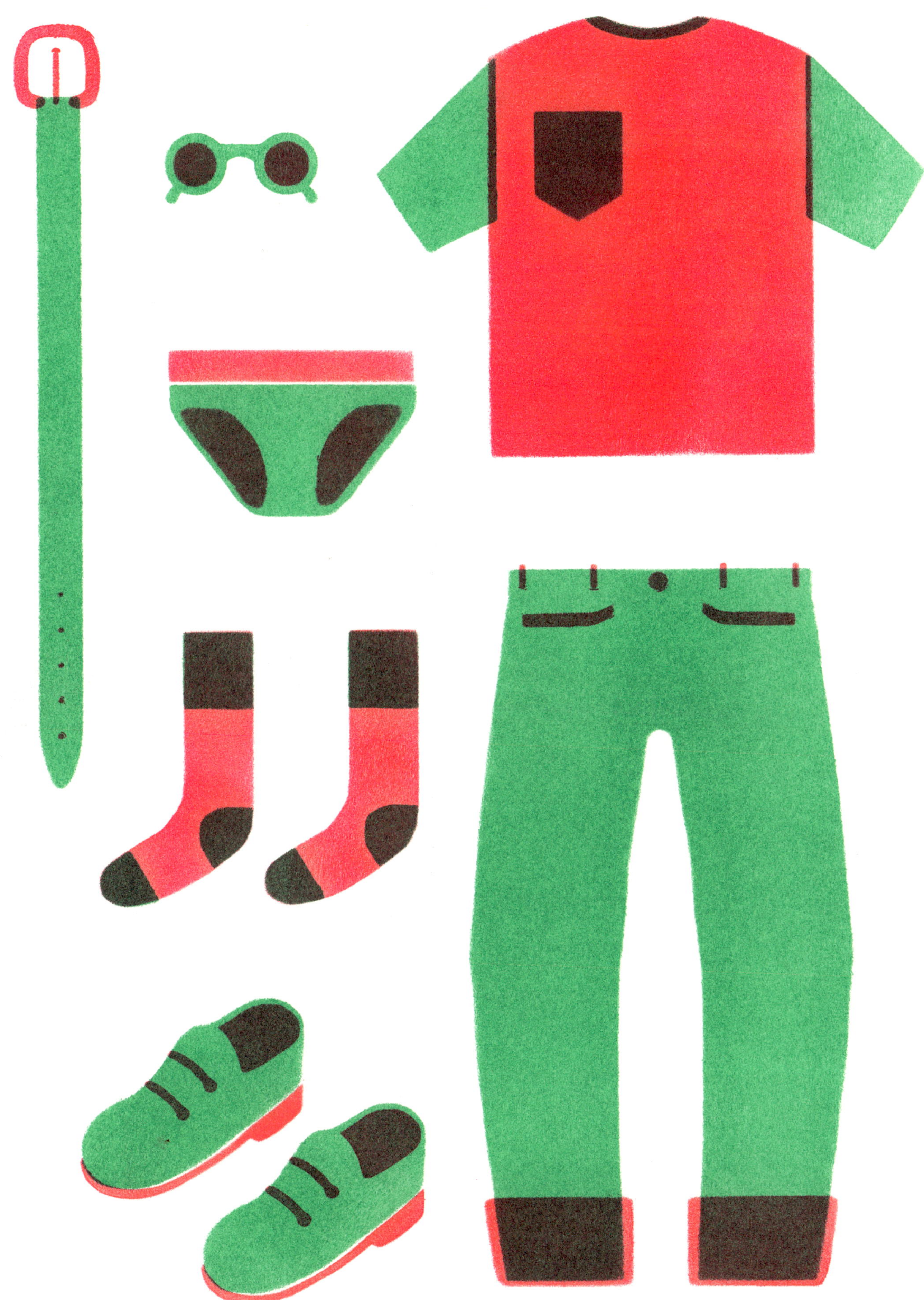

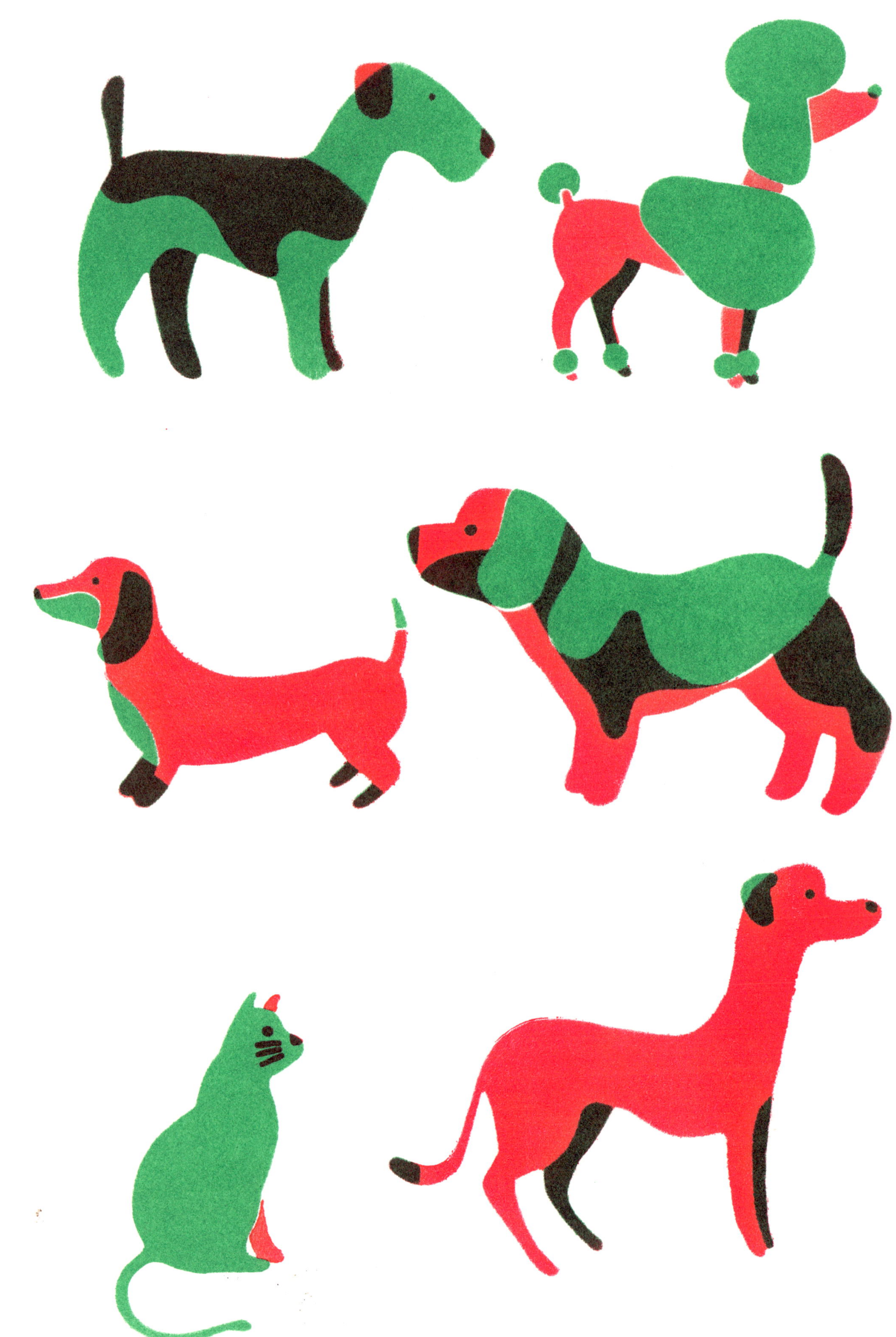

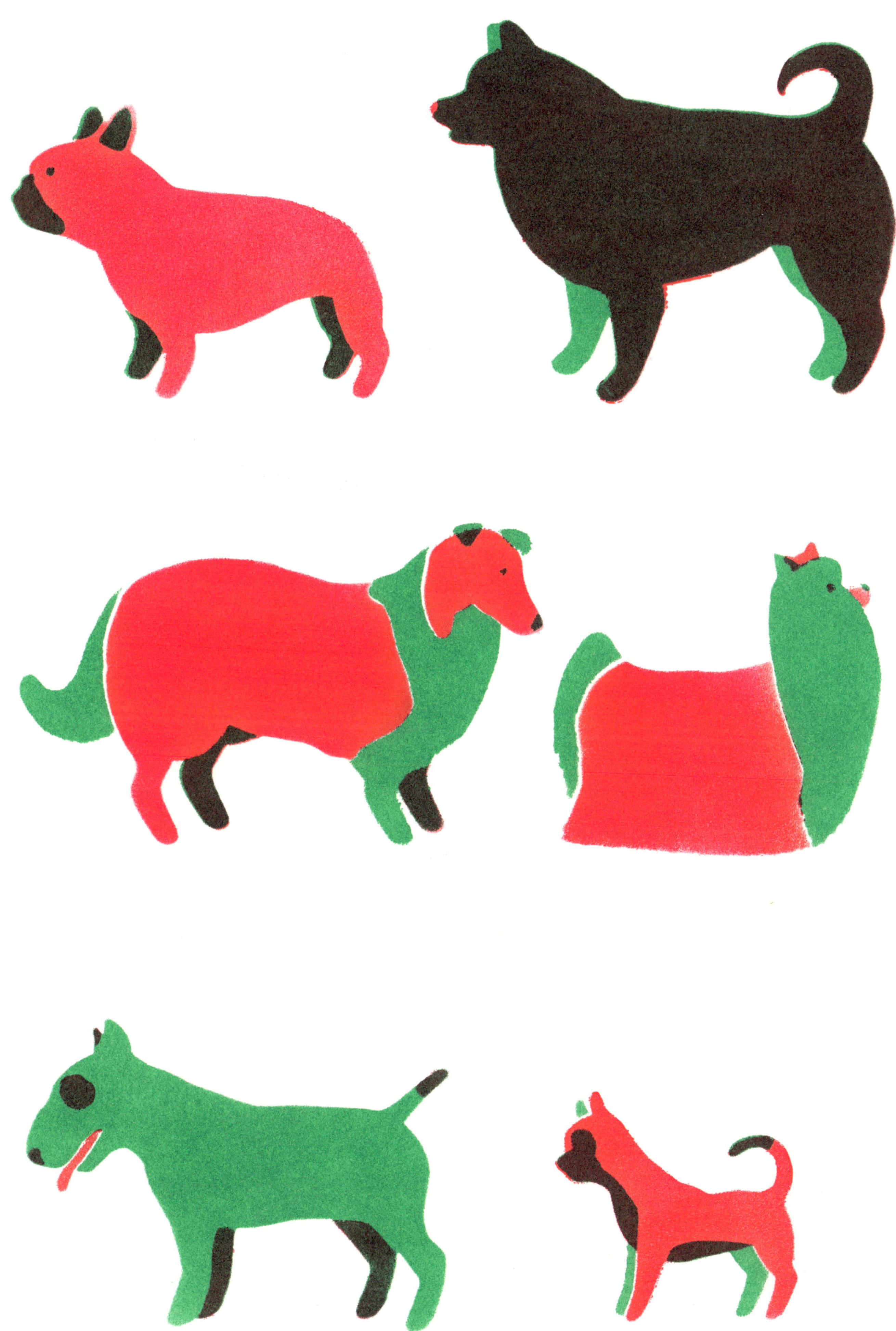

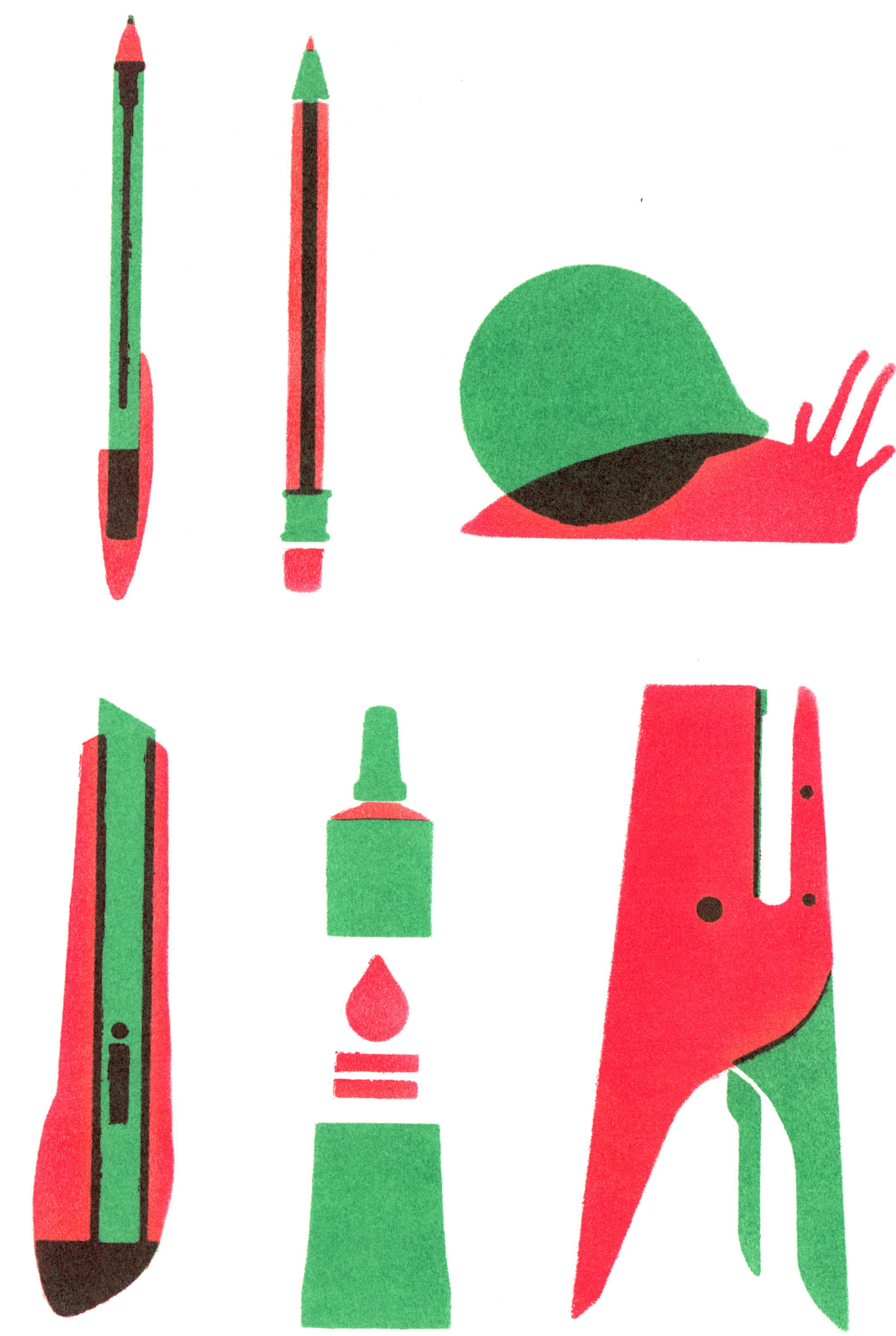

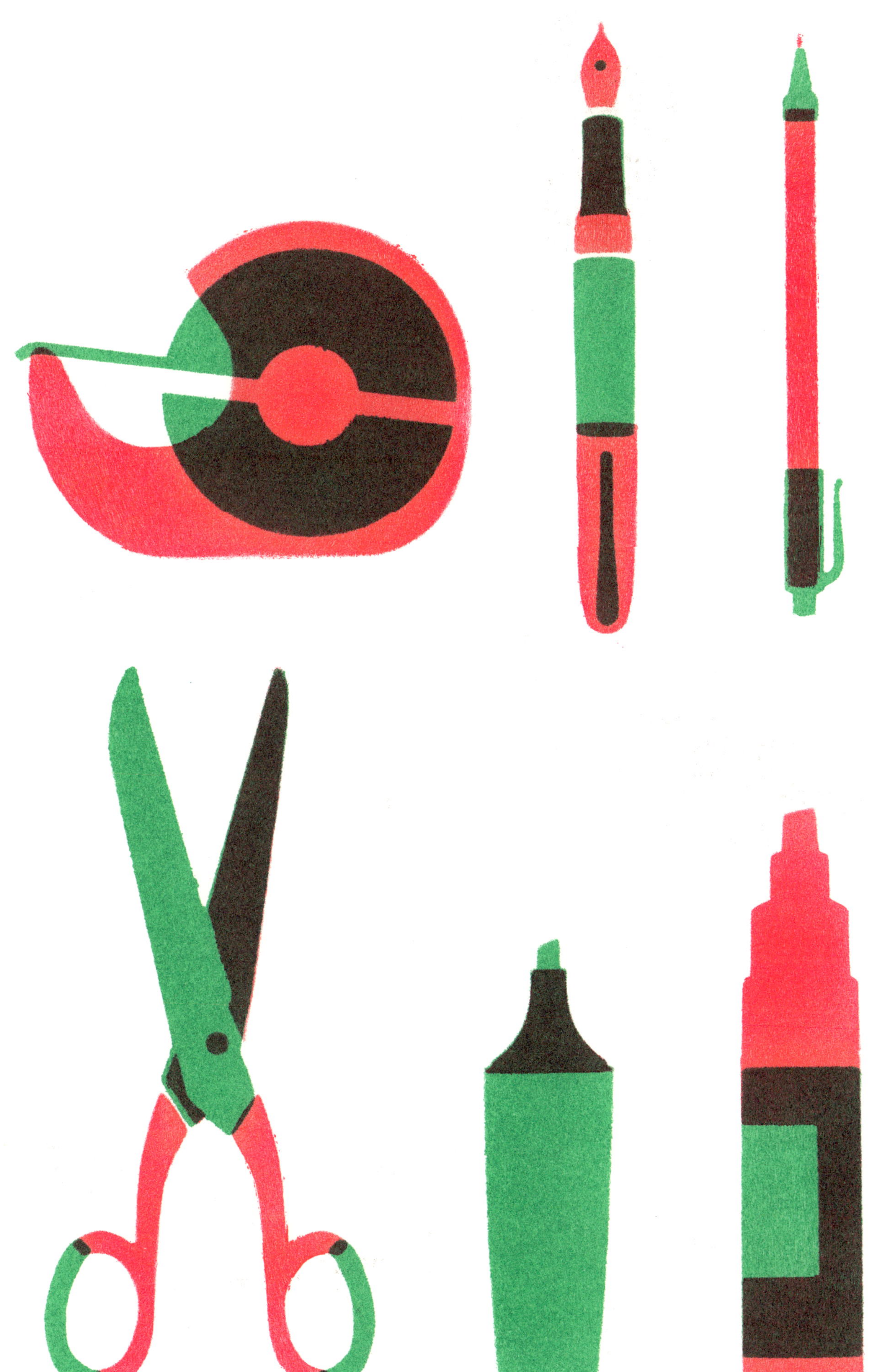

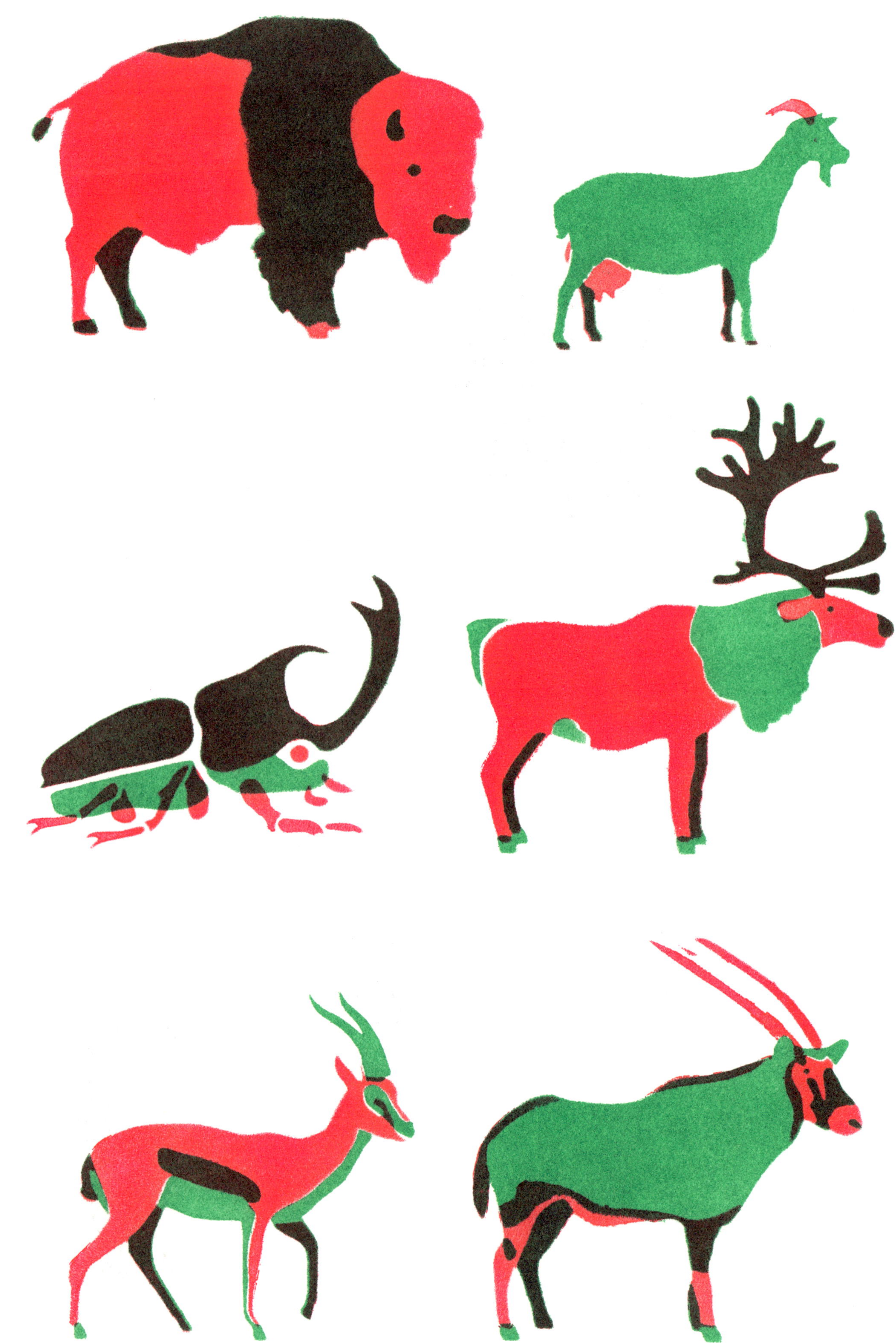

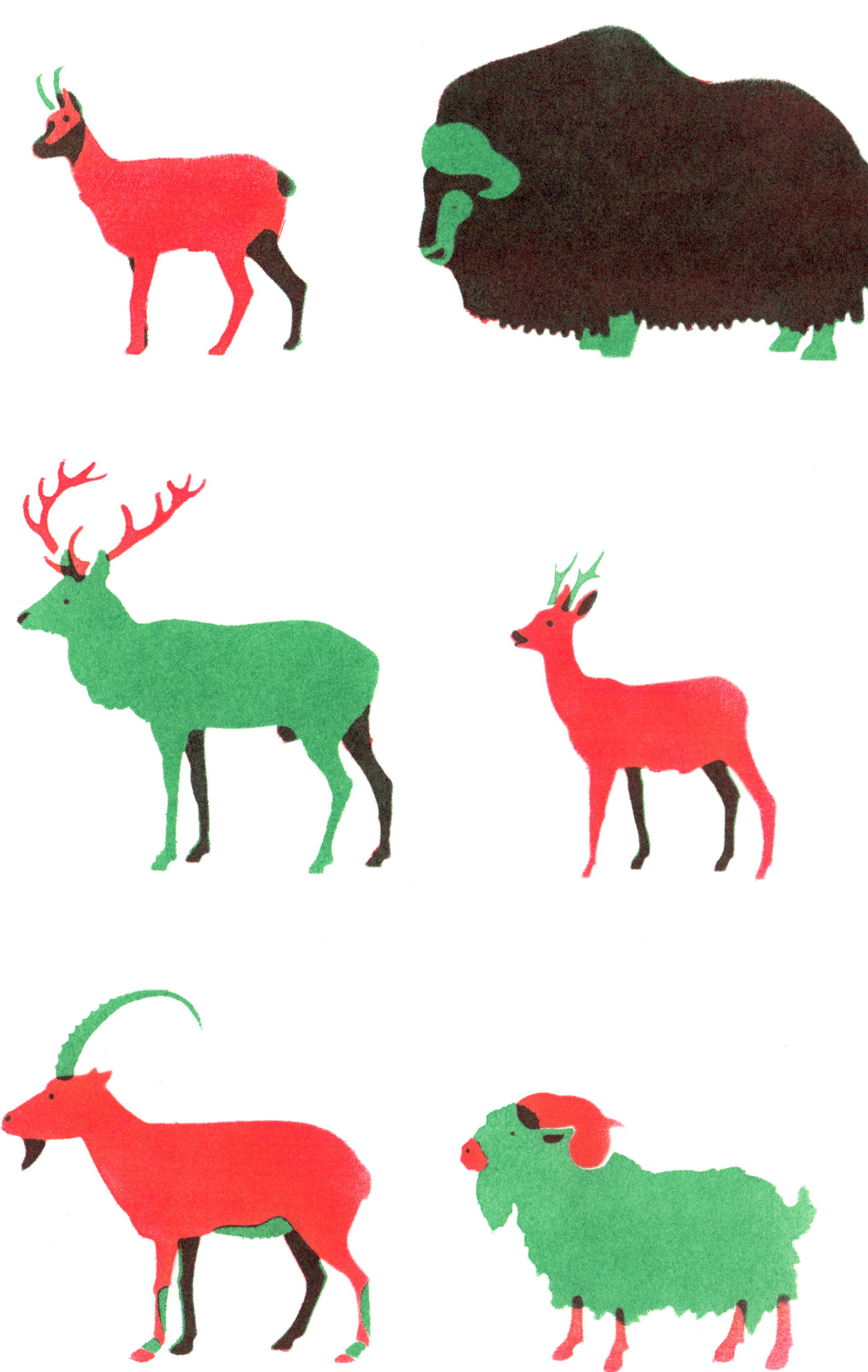

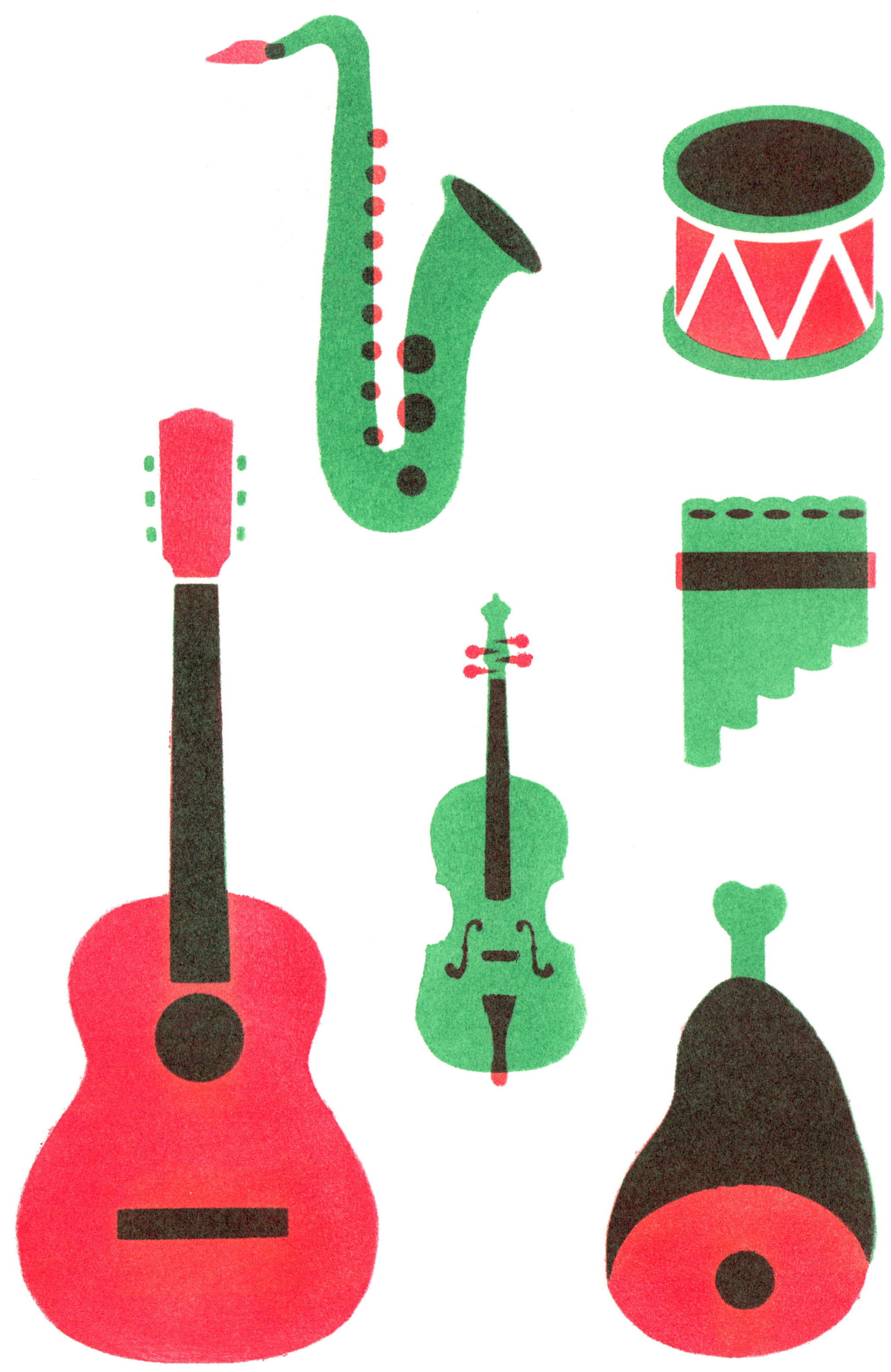

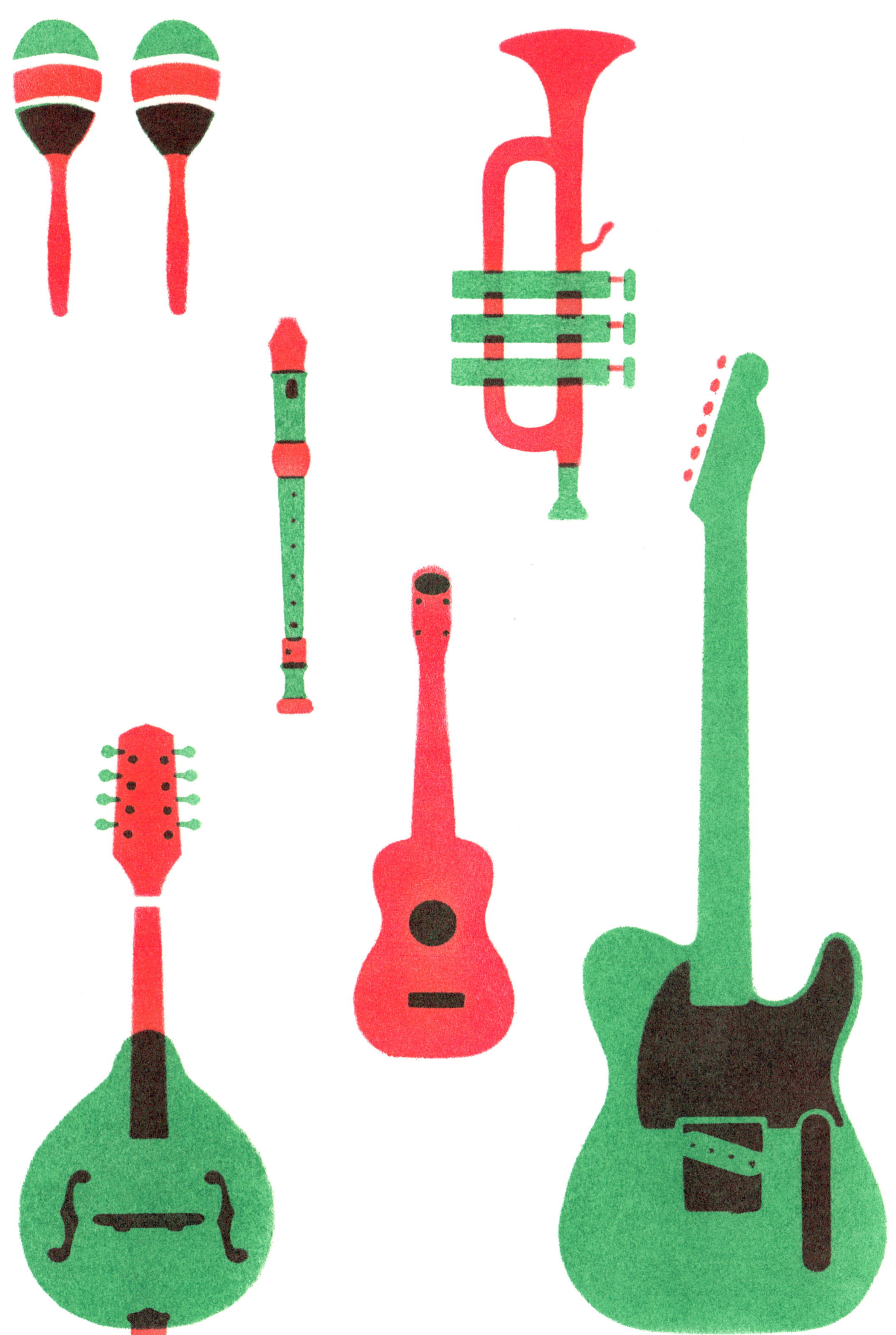

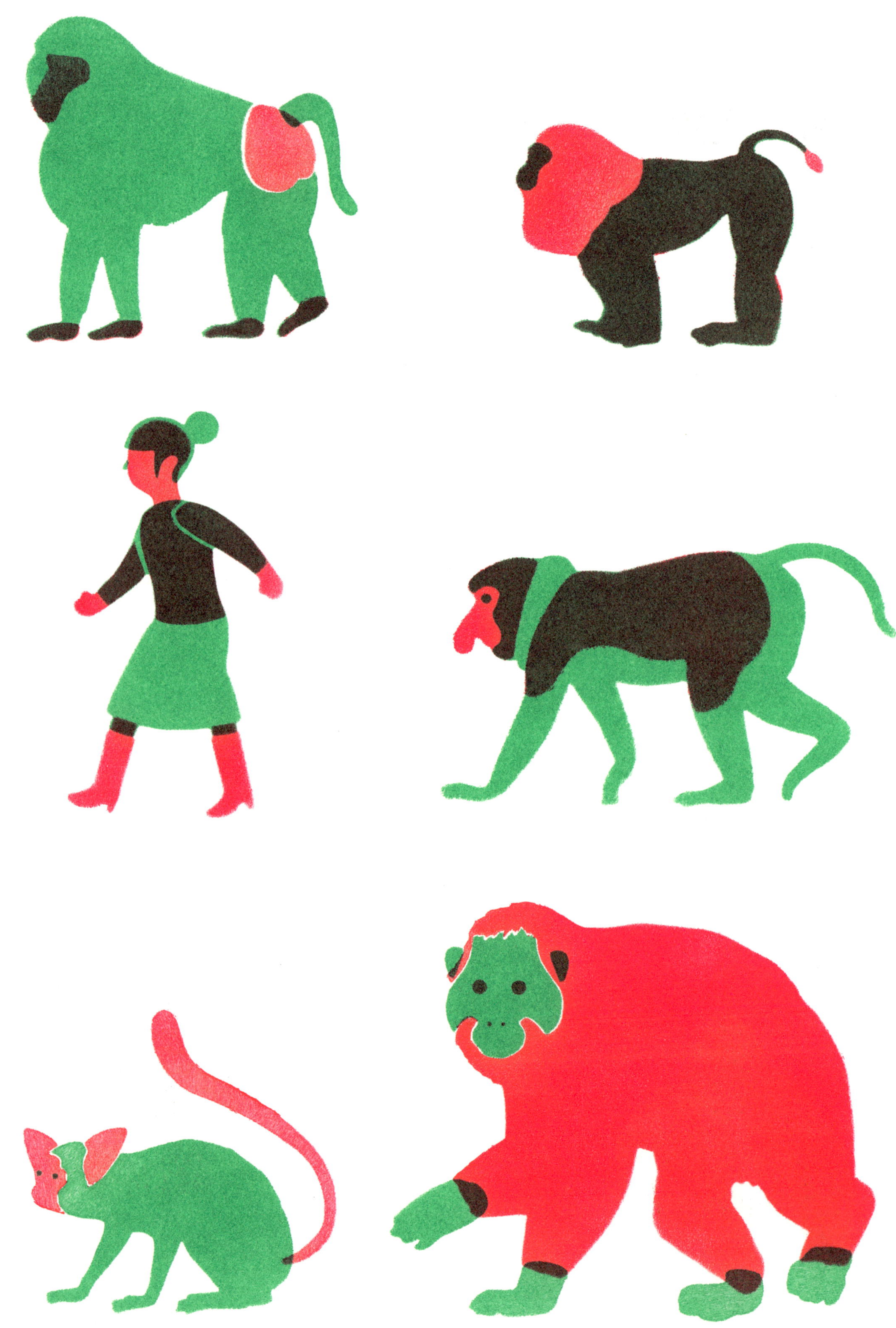

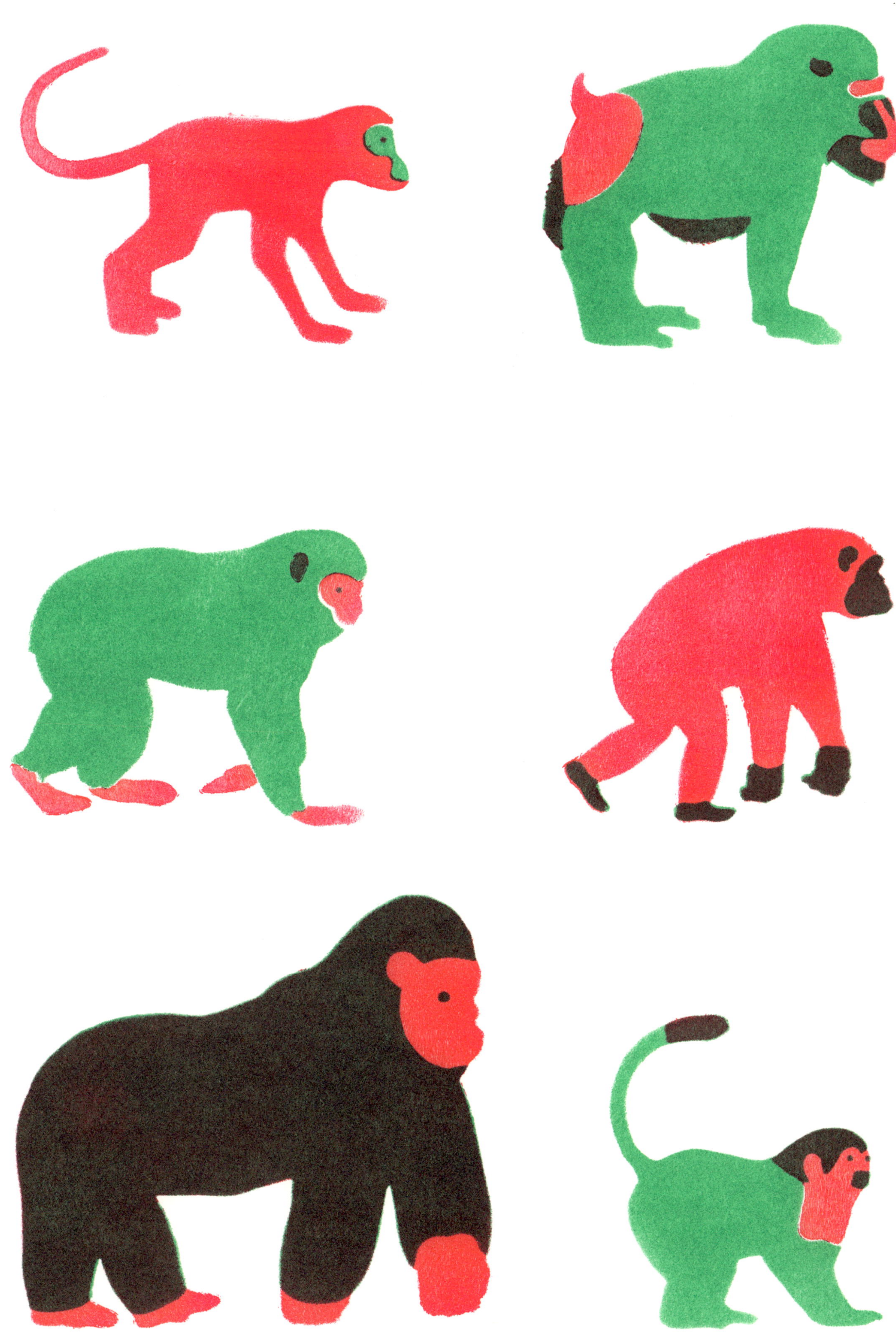

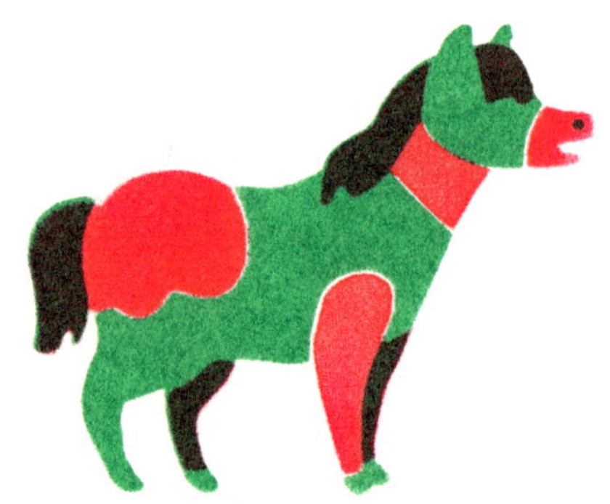